W9-CFF-043

HOW WILL WE WRITE THE FINAL CHAPTER OF AMERICA'S "VIETNAM EXPERIENCE"?

I found myself digging into a footlocker full of memories, dragging them out, dusting them off, and asking questions about the land I trod over as a young second lieutenant:

- Today, are the old battlefields I knew so well—Khe Sanh, Con Thien, Mai Loc—like other battlefields of other wars, transformed into peaceful countrysides and quaint villages?
- What did the old, dyed-in-the-wool Communists think about the collapse of global communism?
- What about the 2,260 Americans still missing in action in Southeast Asia?
- And what about the accounts of groups working in Vietnam to provide humanitarian assistance, medical aid, and support for the orphans of the war? Who are these people?

"A timely call to action and reconciliation that should be heeded by people of all political stripes."
—*Flint, Michigan Journal*

"This is a generous book by a good man. . . . A testament of love for his men, for his family, and for his enemy."
—Sheldon Vanauken, author of *A Severe Mercy*

HarperSpotlight

ONE MORE MISSION

OLIVER NORTH RETURNS TO VIETNAM

OLIVER L. NORTH

and David Roth

HarperPaperbacks
New York, New York
ZondervanPublishingHouse
Grand Rapids, Michigan
Divisions of HarperCollins*Publishers*

All Scripture quotations, unless otherwise indicated, are taken from the Holy Bible, New International Version ®. NIV ®. Copyright © 1973, 1978, 1984 by International Bible Society. Used by permission of Zondervan Publishing House. All rights reserved.

HarperPaperbacks   *A Division of* HarperCollins*Publishers*
10 East 53rd Street, New York, N.Y. 10022

A hardcover edition of this book was published in 1993 by Zondervan Publishing House, a division of HarperCollins*Publishers*.

Cover photograph by Lyn Cryderman
All interior photos not otherwise credited are by Lyn Cryderman

First HarperPaperbacks printing: December 1994

Printed in the United States of America

HarperPaperbacks, HarperSpotlight, and colophon are trademarks of HarperCollins*Publishers*

❖ 10 9 8 7 6 5 4 3 2 1

For Betsy,
the wind beneath my wings

But they that wait
upon the Lord
shall renew their strength;
they shall mount up
with wings as eagles;
they shall run,
and not be weary;
and they shall walk,
and not faint.
Isaiah 40:31

CONTENTS

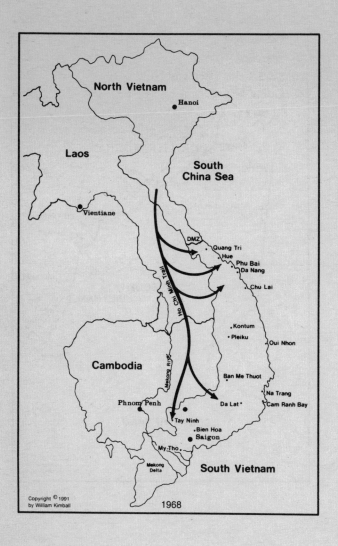

North Vietnam

Hanoi

Laos

South
China Sea

Vientiane

DMZ
Quang Tri
Hue
Phu Bai
Da Nang
Chu Lai

Ho Chi Minh Trail

Kontum
Pleiku
Oui Nhon

Cambodia

Mekong River

Ban Me Thuot

Na Trang

Phnom Penh

Da Lat
Cam Ranh Bay

Tay Ninh
Bien Hoa
Saigon

My Tho

Mekong
Delta

South Vietnam

Copyright © 1991
by William Kimball

1968

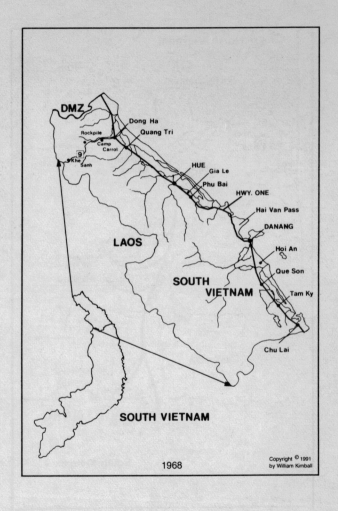

DMZ

Dong Ha
Rockpile
Quang Tri
Camp Carrol
9
Khe Sanh

HUE
Gia Le
Phu Bai
HWY. ONE
Hai Van Pass
DANANG
Hoi An
Que Son
Tam Ky

LAOS

SOUTH VIETNAM

Chu Lai

SOUTH VIETNAM

1968

Copyright © 1991
by William Kimball

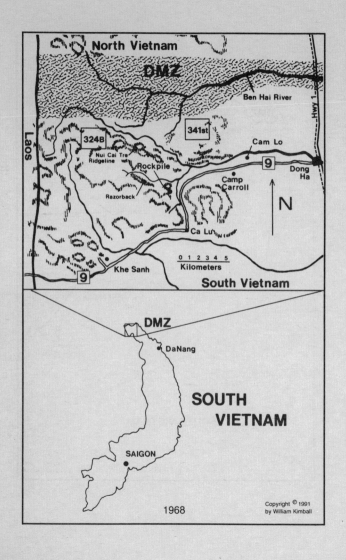

North Vietnam

DMZ

Ben Hai River

Laos

341st

324B

Nui Cai Tre Ridgeline

Rockpile

Razorback

Cam Lo

9

Camp Carroll

Dong Ha

Hwy 1

N

Ca Lu

0 1 2 3 4 5
Kilometers

9   Khe Sanh

South Vietnam

DMZ

DaNang

SOUTH VIETNAM

SAIGON

1968

Copyright © 1991
by William Kimball

ACKNOWLEDGMENTS

HAVING NOW DONE TWO OF THEM, I'VE DECIDED THAT books like this aren't really written—they're built. Any decent-sized building requires the work of many, and this book is no exception. The chapters of this book, like the floors of a multi-storied building, were constructed a page at a time by many people who worked very hard. As the architect, I got to have all the fun.

Ground was broken for this work by Scott Bolinder and Jim Buick at Zondervan Publishing House in Grand Rapids, Michigan. They had the vision to see that which I could not and then followed through to make this idea a reality.

Scott introduced me to David Roth, who brought experience and discipline to this building process. David's expertise and polish were essential ingredients in this final product. Had he not helped me shoulder the load, I would still be at it.

And through Zondervan I also met Ralph Plumb and his team at International Aid, also from the Grand Rapids area. I quickly learned that the good folks at IA—Medical Director Jack Henderson, M.D., Marketing Director Joel Samy, and supporters J. C. Huizenga, Bud Hoffman, and board member Dennis Johnson—know about the hard work of laying bricks and mortar in faraway places. And IA's Vice-President for Operations, Bill Barta, was a major help—even if he did play football at West Point.

Lyn Cryderman, my editor, photographer, and friend, went the extra mile. In fact, he went about 20,000 of them to and from Vietnam and in multiple trips to Washington. His wisdom, advice, and good humor were

xiii

an inspiration to me and everyone who worked on making this *Mission* a success.

About a month into the project, somebody had the bright idea of making a documentary film about Vietnam at the same time that this book was being written. Since doing too many things at once has become a way of life for me, I said: "Why not?"

Zondervan's Executive Producer, Dave Anderson, brought in Steve Zeoli and Intaglio Productions, and they built a team that included co-producer Peter Larson, and two of the best cameramen in the business: Heinz Fussle and Jack Pagano. How they managed to make order out of chaos, employ my meager talent, and create such a great film is beyond me. But they did. And the results are like a warm hearth to a cold heart in the middle of a Michigan winter.

Zondervan didn't stop at hiring half of Michigan for this project. They created an international effort that spanned half the globe and the length and breadth of America. Thus, an effort to express my gratitude reads like a travelogue:

In New York

Jim Fox and Rick Horgan at HarperCollins helped get the project rolling and to keep us on track. The Office of the Vietnamese Delegation to the United Nations, and Elisa Tamarkin of the Office of the U.N. High Commissioner for Refugees assisted us in breaking through a bureaucracy that needs a good Federal Paperwork Reduction Act.

In Washington

United States Senators John McCain and Bob Smith and their staffs provided timely and critically needed advice and encouragement for my trip back to Vietnam. At the Pentagon, the staff in the office of former Chairman of the Joint Chiefs of Staff, General John W. Vessey, helped us avoid complicating his delicate mission. And at my favorite law firm, Williams and Connolly, Nicole Seligman and Brendan Sullivan tried like the dickens, once again, to keep me out of trouble.

In Virginia

My business partner, Joe Fernandez, and our faithful team at Guardian Technologies International, Inc., The Life-Saving Company, provided the encouragement to keep at it when the going got tough. Bouakeo Bounkong and her family inspired me with their courage in starting life over in this blessed land of ours. Marsha Fishbaugh, my dedicated secretary, somehow succeeded in keeping this whole book and video project—and me—on schedule.

Retired Marine Lieutenant General Ed Bronars, Ron Humphries of Prison Fellowship Ministries, the U.S. Marine Corps Historical Center, and the Center for Military History all helped me to fill in critical information gaps. Mark Brender and Jack Pagano provided essential logistics support.

In Virginia Beach, former South Vietnamese Army Colonel Loi helped me see the challenges that Vietnam faces today from a new perspective. And retired Marine Major General John S. Grinalds, now the Headmaster at Woodberry Forest School in Orange, Virginia, and still my favorite Centurion, provided prayer and good counsel in the final phases of construction.

Elsewhere in the USA

Vets With a Mission president and founder, Bill Kimball, in California, and VWAM Chairman of the Board, Roger Helle, in Iowa, have forged the neatest Army-Marine Corps joint operation I've seen in a long time. These men, once on the cutting edge of combat, have become experts at rebuilding broken walls. Nehemiah would have put these guys to work.

Chief researcher Tanya Bartlett and the reference librarians of the University of Arkansas were better at digging through tons of data than Marines are at digging foxholes.

When the call went out to lend a hand at putting this all together, old (and I *do* mean *old*!) Marine comrades came running to help: Paul Goodwin from Ohio; Bill Haskell from Maryland; Jim Lehnert from Chicago; Richmond O'Neill from California; Bud Flowers from Virginia; Ross Petersen from Minnesota; Eric Bowen from New York, and Art Vandaveer from Texas.

In Hanoi

Building this book took more than old friends. It took the help of old adversaries as well. In what was once an enemy capital, we had the aid of Professor Nguyen Trong Nhan, M.D., Minister of Health, Socialist Republic of Vietnam; Nghiem Xuan Tue, Deputy Director, Department of International Relations, Ministry of Labor, Invalids and Social Affairs; and Dr. Nguyen Ba Duc, Director, National Cancer Institute.

Joy My Lien Degenhardt, Vietnam Program Director, Maine Adoption Placement Service, assisted us in finding our way through the maze. Mr. Vinh, our "keeper" in Hanoi, helped us make sure that we got to where we needed to go.

The men and women of Detachment 2, Joint Task Force – Full Accounting, Hanoi, and their commander, Lieutenant Colonel Jack Donovan, U.S.A., were gracious and helpful. Their sincere devotion to a difficult task is obvious. They also make the best burgers and hot dogs north of the Ben Hai River.

In Quang Tri

We benefited from the courtesy of Nguyen Min Ky, Permanent Deputy Chairman of the People's Committee, Quang Tri Province; Bui Dang Quang, M.D., Director of Health Service of Quang Tri Province, Dong Ha; Dr. Nguyen Ngoc Hieu, Director, Trieu Hai Regional Hospital, Quang Tri Province;

Pham Sy Dan, M.D., Director, Quang Tri Provincial Hospital, and Dr. B. V. Tinh, Chief of Pediatrics, Quang Tri Provincial Hospital.

In Ho Chi Minh City

Professor Trinh Kim Anh, M.D., Director, Cho Ray Hospital and Tropical Diseases Research Center, and Chief, Department of Internal Medicine, University of Medicine, Ho Chi Minh City; Nguyen Dich, M.D., Professor of Cardiology and Deputy Director, Cho Ray Hospital and Tropical Disease Research Center; La Van Thien, Director, Amerasian Transit Center, all provided us with critically needed information and courteous help.

In Dong Ha

Former NVA officers, Lieutenant Colonel Le The Danh, Lieutenant Colonel Hoang Kim Dien, Major Ta Quang Thanh, Major Tran Thanh Toan, took the time to sit down with a former adversary to share "war stories" and had the grace at parting to express their admiration for the Marines with whom I had served.

In Da Nang

Father Anthony Nguyen, pastor of the Da Nang Catholic Church, and the people of his parish reminded us that the Holy Spirit is, in spite of everything, alive and well in the first Vietnamese city I saw twenty-five years ago. I will be forever grateful to Mr. Ho Vietine, the Director of the Hoi An Orphanage, for demonstrating to me once again, the magnificent effect of love on a small child and the remarkably resilient human spirit that our Maker put in *all* His creatures. Our trip was greatly assisted by Dr. Nguyen Van Ly and Mr. Nguyen Dinh An.

In Central Vietnam

Our "keepers"—Truong Hao, Nguyen Quang, Bui Thanh Song, Le Bon, Phan Ngoc Luong, Hoang Hoa, and Tran Khanh Phoi—made us all realize, without really trying to, that there are redeeming qualities in those we once fought against.

Elsewhere "In Country"

Michael Viola Vu of Bethany Christian Services was a valuable resource and helped steer us clear of several potential potholes and "minefields" during the course of our travels. There are many other Vietnamese who cannot be thanked in this book, but who have my gratitude in anonymity: the pastors and laypeople of the underground church and the newly released "veterans" of the "reeducation" camps we met with in Vietnam. And, of course, many gracious people we met in Vietnam whose names were simply never noted.

On the Home Front

As she has before, Mom waded through piles of old letters and photos, provided a great humorous incident, and turned seventy-five—all part of helping me finish this book. Thanks, Mom.

The most important people in my life, my best friend, Betsy, and our four children: Tait, Stuart, Sarah, and Dornin, once again tolerated my absences, late nights of writing and phone calls, and visits from all over the earth as I worked to finish. Their prayers, patience, grace, and understanding were the most important building materials I had available.

To the extent that a building stands straight and square, it is because so many cared so much about its outcome. So, too, it is with this book. If a building has deficiencies in the results, they are the fault of the architect. And in this book, any inadequacies or imperfections are solely mine, for I am still a frail, flawed mortal—and a better Marine than an architect.

PROLOGUE

Vietnam: 23 April 1993

THE RAIN STARTED GENTLY, JUST A FEW SMALL DROPS at a time, nothing like I remembered it. The rain in my memories came in torrential downpours, beating down out of dark clouds, hard against the skin, hard enough to hurt. But this rain was delicate, a mist from billowing white clouds that cast their dancing shadows on the lush, verdant valley below.

I peered down from the roadside ledge where we had stopped. A farmer wearing a wide, conical straw hat was following a water buffalo as he guided his plow through a rice paddy, preparing it for planting. A village of thatched roofs could be seen in the distance among the palms.

Behind the houses I didn't remember, I recognized a small river, its course unchanged over the

1

quarter century since I had last stood on this spot. But it, too, was different. The echoing laughter of children playing under a waterfall floated up to us softly, like the rain, as I stood watching. They were having a water fight. How different from the fights I remembered here so long ago.

If I hadn't been here before, if I didn't have so many memories of this valley and the mountains beyond, I would have thought it was Shangri-la. But James Hilton's idyllic refuge had always been peaceful. This valley hadn't.

Back in 1968 there were no children laughing and playing in the river. There were no farmers tilling fields. No houses. Only U.S. Marines and soldiers. And the North Vietnamese Army, of course.

I was standing on the crest of a hill beside the road to Khe Sanh, looking into the Dakrong River Valley. To the north, the jungle-covered mountains that had once been the border between two countries were still where I remembered them, but the line through those mountains that had showed only on our maps back then, with its "demilitarized zone" dividing the two Vietnams, was gone forever.

Twenty-five years ago I had walked and fought over these green hills, clad in an armored flak jacket and the jungle camouflage of the U.S. Marines. Then, we walked nearly everywhere we went. Occasionally we rode in armed helicopters or tanks or heavily armored military vehicles, all of them the same flat olive-drab.

Now, in April of 1993, I had come back to walk the same battlefields where so many had bled and died. This time my companions and I were wearing comfortable sports clothes, riding in air-conditioned, white vans and civilian jeeps. And they weren't Marines.

Instead of M-16 rifles, machine guns, grenade launchers, and tactical radios, we were carrying video recorders, cameras, and medical supplies. We had come back to the much-tortured land of Vietnam to chronicle the changes that had taken place since I had served there.

We had come because America's new president, Bill Clinton, said that he wanted to "normalize" relations with the now-united Vietnam. With more than 2,200 Americans still missing in Southeast Asia, stories of political and religious repression persisting, and continuing reports of Vietnamese troops in neighboring Cambodia and Laos, there is a growing controversy over just such a possible course of action.

We had come to see firsthand what other Americans—many of whom were veterans like me—were doing there. I had heard that they were there trying to finish something that America had started so very long ago. I had heard that they were in Vietnam, not using the tools of war but bandages and antibiotics and prosthetic limbs; not at the direction of government but at the urging of their souls. I wanted to see this for myself.

After several days of hard travel our trip had brought us to this remote valley I remembered so well but so differently. We stood there in the quiet, the sun setting peacefully behind us over the Khe Sanh battlefield. Through the moisture the sun's rays cast a rainbow that appeared over the valley. One of our Vietnamese "guides" approached and broke the spell. He was a member of the local

People's Committee and was serving as one of our translators for this part of our journey.

"It is very beautiful, isn't it?" he asked.

"Yes, it is," was all I could say.

"You fought here, didn't you?" he probed further.

"Yes, I did."

"Did you lose many friends here?

"Yes."

"I know a tribute to them. Would you like to hear it?"

I was at once curious and skeptical. Why did this gentle, delicate, little man want to offer a tribute to my friends who had died here? His own family had fought on the side of the Viet Cong during The War. Was this going to be yet another "anti-imperialist" diatribe at the cost of my fallen friends and countrymen? Cautious but intrigued, I said, "Yes, please."

He began, in hushed tones and flawless English: "Four score and seven years ago, our fathers brought forth on this continent a new nation. . . ."

His recitation was faultless to the end. Well before Nguyen finished those stirring words first uttered at Gettysburg 129 years before, there were tears streaming down my cheeks. Lincoln's aim was to heal a broken nation. His words were offered as a eulogy to the brave men on both sides who died on the Pennsylvania battlefield where he spoke. Now, on this mountainside, half a world away, not far from the site of one of Vietnam's bloodiest battles, a former enemy was repeating the Gettysburg Address better than many school children in my own country could.

"How did you learn that?" I asked after he had finished.

"From your Voice of America," he replied.

In Lincoln's Address is the beginning of this book. The warriors I served with in Vietnam never got such an accolade. The heroes who fought there were never so recognized; the parents, wives, children, and beloved of those who served received scant thanks from most of the nation. The anguish of those who lost fathers, sons, husbands, and brothers, wives, daughters, and sisters in the only war America ever lost has barely been acknowledged. For those who still wait for word of a loved one missing somewhere in Southeast Asia, there is little patience or appreciation. Those who agonized over Vietnam have never had a chance to put "The War" behind them. For many of us, America's longest war continues to be the war that refuses to end.

This a book about war. But it is much more than a war story. The accounts of battle in this narrative are included because they are etched indelibly in my memory. They have shaped and sharpened who I am, how I feel about Vietnam and those who endured that experience.

For two-and-a-half decades, the most vivid recollections I had of Vietnam were those of combat, bloodshed, and thankless, heroic sacrifice. My return to those old battlefields melted this frozen snapshot and offered a new perspective of that ordeal.

These experiences, then and now, and the lessons drawn from them, are offered as a tribute to those who served, those who waited, those who lost a loved one, and those who still wait for word of one missing in that long ago war.

If you are one of them—if you are one of us—this book is for you.

PART I
THE WAR

I

"KILO ONE ACTUAL IS DOWN"

Vietnam: 25 May 1969

KILO ONE ACTUAL IS *DOWN*. WE NEED HELP!" THE radio handset in Jim Lehnert's hand crackled. Over the firing I could hear the voice of Sergeant Jose Cruz, the 1st Platoon's Guide. "Kilo Six, Kilo Six, this is Kilo One Golf. Kilo One Actual is down. We need help in a hurry. We've got five or six wounded. I need . . ." and the radio went dead.

Bill Haskell—1st Platoon Commander, Company K, 3d Battalion, 3d Marine Regiment, 3d Marine Division,—"Kilo One Actual"—was hit in the opening burst of fire. The crack of the AK-47s from our right front was followed immediately by exploding rifle-fired and rocket-propelled grenades, or RPGs. Then came the louder reports of a heavy machine gun as it cut a swath through the trees just

9

above our heads. *Ambush*, I thought. I started yelling for my third squad, right behind me, to move up on the right, envelop the enemy's flank, and cut off their inevitable withdrawal.

My mind raced. Something was terribly wrong. Haskell couldn't be hurt. He'd been at this longer than any of the rest of us. He's the one who taught me how to "break brush." He was the one the Company Commander called on when he wanted to move fast, because Haskell was the toughest of all his lieutenants. Haskell had survived innumerable ambushes—both ours and theirs. For more than six months Bill Haskell, Rich O'Neill, and I had been like brothers—at times we'd been the only officers in this rifle company. Now, Rich had moved up to the Division Battalion staff, leaving Haskell and me as Kilo Company's two longest surviving officers. We were good and we knew it. Most important, our Marines knew it, and that made all the difference in the world.

From the moment I'd arrived in Vietnam, over six months before, Haskell had helped me hone the patrolling and ambush skills that had been drummed into us at Quantico. A few weeks before, his first platoon had conducted one of the biggest ambushes of the war, for which many of his men had been decorated for heroism. Bill had, quite properly, been awarded the Silver Star.

Earlier that day, May 25, 1969, well before dawn, Captain Paul Goodwin, the Commanding Officer of Company K—Kilo Company—3d Battalion, 3d Marine Regiment, had summoned his officers to a hasty conference beneath a poncho, where he gave us our assignments.

Stabbing a dirty finger at the map on the ground, Goodwin said, "In the morning we're going to move up to the top of Mutter's Ridge on the DMZ. Before dark we need to be here," he said, pointing to Hill 410, at 1,330 feet the highest terrain feature on that part of the so-called demilitarized zone that divided North and South Vietnam.

"The S-2 at Battalion says that there is a lot of sensor activity from the top and the north slope, possibly 2 NVA regiments in the area between the Ben Hai River and the southern border of the Z. Lima Company will be on our left, Mike Company is here with the Battalion CP group. India Company is here.

"After we get on top, we'll set up a Company Patrol Base and send two fifteen-man teams into the DMZ for a day to capture some NVA prisoners and assess how long they have been there and where they're heading.

"Bill, I want your platoon to take the point this morning. Second platoon is pooped from breaking brush yesterday, and besides Blue has dysentery again. (They called me "Blue," a nickname derived from our brevity code name for the compass direction "north.") I don't want to have to stop every time he needs to."

Goodwin went on and gave assignments to the rest of the Company. Lieutenant Art Vandaveer, the artillery Forward Observer, and Sergeant Getze, the Forward Air Controller, were told to stay close to Goodwin and the Company command group. By mid-afternoon that would prove to be a life-saving decision for all of us.

In those days a full-strength Marine rifle company

numbered 210 men. A total complement of officers would have given us a captain as company commander, a first lieutenant as executive officer or "XO," and four second lieutenants to command the three rifle platoons and the weapons platoon. Out in the bush for protracted periods, we would also have attached engineers, artillery spotters, forward air controllers, and, of course, corpsmen to care for the wounded.

But as usual, the company wasn't up to full strength. At the beginning of May we had assembled at Con Thien Combat Base, our battalion's "home away from home," long enough to receive replacements and refit worn equipment. Enough BNGs—brand-new guys—had joined to bring us up to nearly full strength. But that was a lifetime ago. Since then, we had been on patrol, then back into Con Thien, loaded aboard a heavily armed convoy for the rough ride down Route 9 to The Rockpile, the 3d Marines Regimental Command Post, and after the ride, back again to our most reliable form of transportation—our feet. For twenty days the company had been walking and fighting its way north toward the ominous ridgeline that towered above us.

By the morning of May 25, 1969, Company K, 3d Battalion, 3d Marines was down to four of seven officers and 159 Marines—51 short of our full complement. Those who were no longer with us hadn't all disappeared at once, of course. They left as they usually did in this strange war—in ones and twos. A number were wounded. Others got malaria, or dysentery, or one of the many strange tropical diseases that seemed to flourish in

Vietnam. Occasionally there was a severe case of heat stroke.

Some were carried off in body bags.

Every once in a while a Marine would come up to his platoon leader in the last moment of daylight as the unit was digging in for the night and quietly whisper: "Lieutenant, just a reminder—I go back to 'The World' in three days. Can I have Jones take my place on point tomorrow?" We all tried to get those guys back to the rear and relative safety in Quang Tri on the next available helo.

The fact that our rifle company had lost twenty-five percent of its strength hadn't changed our mission a bit. When we had walked north from The Rockpile at the beginning of May, our task was to clear North Vietnamese Army units from the mountainous, jungle-covered ridges south of the DMZ. None of us expected that we would be entering the four-mile-wide zone that separated the two Vietnams. Now, footsore, hot, tired, and in some cases sick and hurt, we were being given a new mission.

For weeks the 3d Marine Division Headquarters at Dong Ha had been passing down to its nine infantry battalions, sensitive and alarming intelligence reports about how the North Vietnamese Army planned to take advantage of the recently started Paris peace talks to seize territory in South Vietnam as a "bargaining chip" in a settlement. By late May 1969, U.S. and Republic of Vietnam military planners were convinced that several large NVA units were digging in south of the border separating the two countries.

They were also persuaded, as we were, that a significant show of force by well-armed and well-supported Marine and U.S. Army units would force the NVA back to the north. Everyone expected that the elusive invaders would, as they had so many times before, simply give us some token resistance and then fade back across the border. We couldn't have been more wrong.

Shortly after dawn, "Haskell's Rascals," as first platoon referred to itself, eased quietly off the little hilltop where the company had spent the night and began working their way up the finger jutting down from the ridge looming high above us. My second platoon fell in behind, with Goodwin's command group and its "antenna farm" dropping in behind my third squad. Third platoon, providing flank and rear security, was forced by the terrain and vegetation to close in on the main column.

For almost five hours we slogged away, closing in on the steeper elevations that led to Hill 410 on the southern border of the DMZ. Bill's platoon was setting a good pace, and Goodwin was pleased because as long as something didn't go wrong—if we didn't have a heat casualty or enemy contact, or something worse—we might well be able to make the crest of the ridge by mid-afternoon. That would give us plenty of time to set up a strong position, dig in, and send out patrols to fend off the inevitable probes and counterattacks from an evasive enemy that seemed to be able to appear and disappear at will.

Only a fool or a totally BNG—a "brand-new guy"—failed to respect our adversaries. You did so at your own peril. The North Vietnamese

Army—the NVA regulars we encountered in these jungle-carpeted hills—were well-trained, well-equipped, tenacious, and thoroughly committed to winning the war.

By the time I got to Vietnam in 1968, everyone "in country" knew from debriefed NVA prisoners that the enemy didn't expect to win every battle. They simply wanted to win the war—no matter how long it took. They also believed that if they were able to inflict enough casualties on the Americans who were doing most of the fighting in the northern part of the Republic of Vietnam that we would eventually lose the will to continue the fight. After all, they reasoned, the new president, Richard Nixon, had won the election on the promise of ending our involvement in what had already become America's longest war.

To those of us doing the fighting it sometimes seemed that our enemies didn't care how many casualties they took. In our hearts we knew better, but I often wondered what kind of leadership they must have had to be willing to sacrifice so many of their young men in what, at the time, seemed to be fruitless battles. Every engagement I witnessed inflicted higher casualties on them than they did on us. But at the time, I misunderstood the fundamental difference between our two sides. We were fighting not to lose. They were fighting to win.

On our side, we simply wanted to survive thirteen months "in the bush" and make it—alive and in one piece—back to "The World," "the good ol' U.S. of A.," "The Fam," "The Little Woman." In other words, *home*. The NVA went to war to finish what they had started, with no "rotation date," no "end-of-tour," no "world" to go back to. They regarded us as aggressors, not saviors, and were committed to driving us out of Vietnam just as they had driven out the French a decade and a half before. For us, success was defined by the "body count" ratios after each contact. For them, it was all a matter of time.

And it was time that was driving us that morning as our column of aptly named "grunts" struggled and strained up the slope like a long, green, armed and sweating centipede. Goodwin was determined to get us to the crest of the ridge in time to dig some decent holes as protection from the enemy's big guns in North Vietnam. That was always the problem near the DMZ. Once spotted by an NVA forward observer, you could expect everything from mortar fire to 122mm rockets and even barrages of Soviet-made 122mm and 152mm artillery fire.

As far as I was concerned, Goodwin's plan made a lot of sense. Trying to fight it out on the ground with a well-trained adversary who is similarly equipped is bad enough. Having to sit unprotected under enemy "incoming"—mortar, rocket, or artillery fire—trying to pull yourself up into your helmet while high explosives and pieces of steel rain down on top of you is nothing short of horrifying. You never seemed to be able to dig a hole deep enough before the mortars hit, so the extra time to dig in would be welcomed.

Until 12:45 things were going about as well as could be expected. The little O-1 spotter plane buzzing around ahead of us periodically swept across the top of Mutter's Ridge and the crest of Hill 410 but reported nothing. We were moving quietly, inching up the spine of a long finger that jutted down from the peak of the ridge when things instantly went from boredom to stark terror.

By this point in my tour I knew to expect the sudden rush of adrenaline and the wave of nausea that came when things suddenly got bad. But experience had also taught me that invariably, even under the most terrifying circumstances, these young Marines would start doing what they'd had drilled into them, what they had seen others do before, the things they knew almost instinctively that would allow them to prevail and survive. In every other contact I'd been in, no matter how badly it started, the situation inevitably turned the way we wanted, the outcome almost assured by superior firepower, air support, better equipment, and better training.

This time things were going very, very wrong. Most ambushes are over in a matter of seconds. The firing ahead was getting louder and more violent. And now it was being punctuated by the crash of 60mm mortar fire from a weapon high up the ridgeline. This meant it wasn't an ambush, after which the NVA soldiers would melt away into the triple-canopied jungle. We'd bumped headlong into something much bigger. The first rounds had come at us from the right front. Now fire was coming from the left as well. Unable to raise anyone from 1st Platoon on the radio, and with the terrible din of firing and explosions making voice commands impossible, I motioned for second squad to cover our left flank and moved forward with third squad behind me.

As we crawled up the slope, the volume of fire directed against us picked up. Inching upward, I could see wounded Marines from 1st Platoon down behind rocks and trees, some trying to return fire, others treating their injured comrades.

Off to the left front the flash of a heavy machine gun was splattering tracer rounds into the dense foliage fewer that twenty meters ahead.

Jim Lehnert, my radio operator, banged me on the shoulder with the radio handset. Goodwin's southern drawl came through the air: "Close up on Haskell and take the lead," he told me. "His whole first squad seems to be down. I've got an air strike on the way. In exactly ninety seconds, mark the front of our position with a smoke grenade. Tell me the color. I want to bring it in as close as we can. Be careful. Stay in touch."

Later on, some of the Marines from what was left of 1st Platoon and my own 3d Squad would comment that I was very brave to rush forward to throw the grenade. But it wasn't bravery that pushed me to act. Two things were very likely to happen if I didn't do exactly as Goodwin had instructed: First, Goodwin would be furious that the smoke grenade was late; second, the 500-pound high-explosive bombs Goodwin had just summoned forth from the heavens would land on us instead of the North Vietnamese dug in farther up the slope. I'd been "in country" long enough to know that both of these outcomes were to be avoided.

I rolled on my side to slip my seventy-pound

pack off my back, fastened up my flak jacket, and made sure I had a round chambered in my shotgun. Cautiously, I slid forward on my stomach to comply with Goodwin's order, and came upon Haskell. 1st Platoon's chief medical corpsman had dragged him behind a rock, little larger than a fifty-five-gallon oil drum, and was trying to treat what was obviously a very serious wound. Bill's entire head was wrapped in battle dressings that were already soaked through with blood. He had been right at the front of the column when he was hit, and the doc, who had been five or six men back, had only been able to drag him about ten meters back from the killing zone. The men from Haskell's lead squad, nearly all of whom were wounded, had established a small semicircle up the hill and around the rock to protect their fallen lieutenant.

Bloody battle dressings were everywhere. Bullets were cutting through the trees and branches just inches above our heads, and occasionally an AK-47 round would strike the rock that was shielding Haskell and his chief corpsman. Unlike the movies, they didn't ricochet with a whine or a zing, they just hit with a flat slap, and splinters of rock would rain down on Haskell's bandaged head. I motioned for Lehnert to stay put and crawled a few feet forward to heave the smoke grenade. As I did so, Lehnert called on the radio to Goodwin, "Smoke's out, Purple!"

As the colorful cloud billowed into the trees around and above us, I scrambled back to the relative safety of the rock where the Doc was working to start an IV on Bill.

The thick smoke from the grenade obscured targets on both sides of the fight and as the firing died, we could hear the high pitched whine of the waiting F-4 Phantom, beginning its descent from high above us. With engines screaming, the big jet rolled in, and as it passed from left to right across our front 200 meters up the hill from the smoke, I hollered into the handset, "Mark! Mark!" meaning that he was right on target.

On that signal, the Air Spotter in the little O-1 circling above us, directed the wingman of the first Phantom to commence his run on the identical flight path and to release his bombs when he was over the spot where the "Mark, Mark!" had been called.

"Everybody down! Air inbound!" The warning was passed, shouted actually, from man to man, but it was an unnecessary command. With the exception of a few BNGs, these Marines didn't need to be told what was going to happen next. The second F-4 was beginning his bomb run, and now the firing to our immediate front died off almost completely. The NVA also knew what this meant and they were doing the same thing we were—trying to crawl into cracks in the ground!

But now, from well up the hill, there came the sound of a heavy .50-calibre machine gun. And we could tell from the sound that it wasn't pointed at us—it was aiming at one of the two F-4 Phantoms.

As the aircraft passed overhead, the NVA gunner kept right on firing the weapon, even as two 500-pound bombs were released and hurtling toward him. The near simultaneous explosions silenced the heavy machine gun and nearly everything else. The blasts showered the crouching Marines with debris, rocks, dirt, branches, and leaves, but the lull it created gave us an opportunity to reorganize and prepare a proper assault up the narrow finger from which Bill's platoon had been ambushed.

As Staff Sergeant Moncayo, my platoon sergeant, passed instructions to this effect to our three squad leaders and their machine gun and rocket teams, I called Goodwin on the radio: "Have the Airdales give us two more hot passes like that farther up the slope. By the time they've finished, we'll be ready to move."

The brief delay for the additional airstrikes gave me a moment to turn back to Haskell, who was beginning to stir.

"How you doing, Rascal?" He couldn't see me, for the battle dressings covered both eyes. Doc, holding the IV bottle above Bill's head with one hand, looked up at me and with his free hand, motioned to me the course of the projectile that had felled my friend: through his eye and out the side of his head. The corpsman, with tears in his own eyes, shook his head slowly and patted Bill's shoulder.

Even with the covering of gore and battle dressings, he looked deathly pale and his hands were blue and twitching by his sides. "Blue, is that you?" Haskell said weakly. "How about a drink of water?" As he lay there on his back, his head propped up on a pack, blood was dripping down through his mustache into his mouth.

"Yeah, I can manage that," and I held my canteen up to his lips. But he couldn't swallow and began to choke. Handing me the IV bottle, Doc grabbed the canteen and wet a gauze pad, which he placed at Haskell's mouth.

After Bill had sucked on it for a second or two, he spit it out and said, "Well, Blue, I guess I won't be going into the Z with you."

"Yeah, well you don't look so bad to me. What's the matter, you get tired of walking point and decide to take a rest?"

A very small grin began on his lips and he said, "You think you can handle it?"

Lord, here he is, shot in the head, maybe dying, and he's still a wise guy, I thought to myself. And, as we had for so many months, I let him have some of the same right back: "Oh, yeah, I can handle it. But if you're just going to sit here on your duff all afternoon, how 'bout letting me have your boots. Mine have just about had it."

"Nope. Can't have my boots. I'm going to need 'em," he shot back.

As he said those words, the last we would exchange for more than seven months, Lehnert crawled over to me. Goodwin was on the radio and wanted to know if we needed a fourth air strike. "Negative. Have 'em make a cold pass, and we'll get up and get moving while Charlie has his head down. They ought to cover the medevac birds, though, just in case there is another .50-cal up there."

Goodwin's response was the kind that made us all simultaneously love and hate the man: "Lieutenant, I'll take care of the medevacs! You get the front end of this lash-up moving 'cause I'm tired of sitting here getting shot at. We're supposed to be in the Z. Get 'em going!"

There was a pause, and then, "And Blue, . . . be careful."

2

OPENING THE FOOTLOCKER

Virginia: May 1993

I WOULD GUESS THAT ANYBODY WHO SPENT ANY time at all in the military, whether it was the Army, Navy, Air Force, Coast Guard, or Marines, ended up with some kind of box or footlocker full of their collected experiences in uniform. For some of us its contents embrace half a lifetime.

One recent Saturday afternoon, I went rifling through my garage, attic, and basement to look for mine. I found it in the basement. When the North family moved to the farm where we now live, it had been buried beneath boxes in a damp corner. I took it to the porch to open.

I had last packed this locker when I was a major in the 3d Battalion, 8th Marines, and I don't think I have opened it but once since then. Inside were

24

maps, notebooks, and letters, a flag I carried throughout my tour in Vietnam, and photographs of, with, and from the guys I served with. The blue boxes that had contained the medals I'd been awarded were buried beneath the maps. These are the things that stir memories. They take us back. For me, this is where, for a quarter-century, I kept Vietnam.

The names of the young Marines I served with, some of whom are on that Wall in Washington, D.C., are scrawled in my pocket-size notebooks. So are the places we went to, the requirements we had for resupply, things like *6 new entrenching tools* and *7 pairs of trousers and twenty pairs of socks*, along with notes to turn in the extra gear and to get five new helmets. A little instruction about enemy snipers was written after a contact in February '69.

Like war itself, my footlocker was full of the mundane. As I looked through my notebooks I discovered entries like these: *No metal canteens. Gas masks not in packs. Canteens must be either in the pack or in a holder. No shiny white objects on the helmets. Stay down when stopped no matter how short. No soda cans on the move. No talking, sleeping in shelters, or moving around.*

We lieutenants usually made notes like these when we were getting orders from the company commander. Sometimes we would write down instructions before briefing our squads or individual Marines. When I needed a resupply, I would make a note of what I needed. Some notes were for briefing the brand-new guys, or *BNGs*, when they arrived—just a little bit of extra instruction. I would guess that the instructions about canteens and not putting the gas mask in a pack were probably for new guys.

There's a note from the 17th of July: *Two Marines being transferred to the 9th Marine Regiment.* I wrote down recommendations for promotion to Lance Corporal at the end of July and recommended that five of my men be awarded medals for heroism. I have tried to recall the details of their particular actions, but I just do not remember the specifics. Like my memory, the writing on the page has faded. Some of the ink has run. The notebooks were frequently wet in the rain and often soaked with sweat.

There's a resupply list written on July 30, two days after a major contact in which Captain Mike Wunsch, a company commander, was killed: *14 flak jackets, 40 fuse lighters, 10 feet of fuse, 5 blasting caps, 8 boxes of C-4 explosive, 65 hand grenades, 30 trip flares, 9 Claymore mines.* The list goes on. *Two cases of M-60 machine-gun ammunition, four crates of M-16 ammo.*

As I paged through my notebooks, I was looking for a complete list of the names of the men in my platoon. I never found it.

I did find a checklist of the required equipment for my rifle platoon, a small catalog of what an individual Marine would carry: an M-60, M-16, or M-79 grenade launcher; an entrenching tool; a radio (PRC-25) for the radio operator and 4 radio batteries (each about the size and weight of a brick); 5 grenades; 2 smoke grenades; a machete; a C/S grenade; a gas mask; 1 illumination round and 1 HE round for the 60mm mortar; 2 bandoliers of M-16 ammunition; 1 bandolier of M-60 machine-gun ammunition; 1 poncho; 1 poncho liner; 1 long-range patrol ration; and 6 C-rations; 5 M-79 rounds for the M-79 man, because he couldn't carry them all.

That's a lot of weight! And they had the nerve to call us *light* infantry!

In your notebook you had to keep the frequencies and radio call signs, code words or brevity codes for grid locations on our maps—"thrust points" as they were called. You would mark those on your map and refer to them by the name rather than their numerical grid locations. That way you could mention them over the radio and even if the enemy was listening, he theoretically could not figure out your location or where you were headed. We didn't have today's high-tech encryption equipment back in those days.

I kept next-of-kin information on Marines in my platoon. And I wrote myself a reminder to let Betsy know about a life-insurance policy. Back then the premium was only $14.65 a month. "No radios or hi-fis or tape players out in the field. Keep quiet on the move. Keep spread out. On halts, alternate your weapons." There's a note to make sure the platoon gets haircuts the next time we go back into Con Thien. There's another note about shaving gear.

An awful lot of Vietnam was just a matter of hiking up one hilltop after another. As I looked back at the maps that had been buried in my footlocker, I realize we went back and forth over much of the same terrain for the better part of a year.

In April and May of 1969, we came and went repeatedly to and from "The Rockpile." The grease pencil on my map shows the routes of platoon- and company-sized patrols along the DMZ. It shows our unit leaving Vandegrift Combat Base, going by The Rockpile and then hiking all the way up into the Demilitarized Zone—the DMZ, or as the troops affectionately called it, "The Z"—itself. In May of '69 we went on an operation into the DMZ to capture NVA troops who were operating close to the South Vietnamese border. It was on that operation, on the 25th of May, that Bill Haskell was so badly wounded.

One of the notes about that operation indicated that the number of people that could go into the Z was limited to two separate fifteen-man patrols!

Somebody in Washington decided that we shouldn't take too many people into the "demilitarized zone." That's one of the problems with the way the whole war was fought. It was guaranteed that you weren't going to be able to win. By 1968 and '69 one of our greatest frustrations was that everybody knew that the war was not going to be won in any conventional sense.

By then we were in the process of what was called "Vietnamization." The idea was simple but unworkable: We would help the Vietnamese enough for them to recruit and train an adequate force to defend their own country. Though the concept was noble, the South Vietnamese fighting a Viet Cong insurgency in their own country and repelling an invasion from the north at the same time was really an impossibility. All of us who served along the demilitarized zone that separated the two countries knew by 1968 that there were an awful lot of North Vietnamese Army soldiers operating in the South. Many of those soldiers didn't even know that they were in South Vietnam. They regarded Vietnam as one country. That's what their political indoctrination taught, the way their maps showed it, and that's the way they saw it. Therefore they didn't have a sense of being invaders. They simply thought they were repelling the American aggressors.

In my whole year over there, we went into the DMZ only twice, once from Con Thien in February 1969 and then once more in May. The demilitarized zone was treated as such by our side. It certainly was not regarded that way by the other side. For the NVA it was just another hill to climb, and they operated with impunity inside and south of the DMZ.

We used to sit and wonder how we could run a B-52 strike one day and then a day later there would be thousands of them—a regimental-size unit or better—attacking some of our emplacements. I never really knew how extraordinary their tunnel complexes were until I went back to Vietnam in 1993. To see the remarkable tunnels of Vinh Moc along the South China Sea was amazing. The Vietnamese boast of how people lived underground and babies were born in tunnel alcoves. Whether or not they exaggerate about how many stayed underground and how long they were there is almost beside the point. What they created was a complex, massive network of passageways, entrances, exits, and airshafts. Once I saw the extraordinary facilities that they created at Vinh Moc, it is no longer hard to comprehend how, in spite of repeated B-52 "arc light bombing," the NVA could reappear in the same area the next day.

They would simply emerge in the dark of night from bunkers that were in some cases 20-25 meters deep, walk across the newly made bomb craters, and ambush our Marines.

On the couple of occasions when we actually entered the DMZ, things were very tense because we were walking right into their base areas. They were well-defended, heavily fortified, and the NVA fought tenaciously to defend them. By the time we actually got into these bases, we would find mere remnants of their having been there—weapons, supplies, and equipment that they left behind. The only way we were able to capture any of them was by aggressively pursuing them deep into the DMZ with small patrols.

On the back of one of my maps I found a letter I had written to my dad. I wrote to him in a way that I didn't write to others. He had served with George Patton's 3d Army in World War II, had survived war himself and knew what it is all about. I could write to him man-to-man and know that he would understand.

The letter on the map had been written right after the May '69 operation that took us inside the DMZ. We had been assigned to bring back a prisoner, preferably an officer, and any intelligence information we could find. Our intent was to prove the NVA presence within the DMZ south of the Ben Hai River, the actual border between South and North Vietnam. We were told to assess the enemy's strengths, the size of the NVA units, and the length of time they had been inside the DMZ. That was best done by capturing some prisoners, but it could also be done by looking at the magnitude of the bunker complexes they had built.

Here is part of the somewhat cryptic letter I wrote Dad:

Teams inserted in the DMZ at 7:00 o'clock on 26 May, moved north for 4 hours. At 11:10 sighted 8-10 NVA moving onto a small hill to the north. Moved to within 30 meters of the group and called in fire to their north, as they started moving closer then after a short firefight took two prisoners. Called for the extraction force to evacuate the prisoners and two of our own wounded, Efthimiou and Cole. One prisoner died on the trip back to the company perimeter.

Our team continued on to the north and found the rest of the bunker complex south of a stream. Reconnoitering the area we found 35 packs, 60 weapons, TNT, box mines, fuses, RPG rounds, ammunition, machine-gun ammo, and grenades. Found 30 reinforced bunkers. We were ordered to retire from the area and ambush the entrances. Alpha team [Corporal Dan Doan and his 14-man patrol] ambushed the river area for the night with negative contact. Morning of the 27th called for extraction force to move into the DMZ to cover the team's movement into the bunker complex. The area was vacant. It had been cleaned out during the windstorm that night. Deployed a seismic intrusion device that would send up a signal to a radio relay site. It would tell when that particular beacon was activated, when there was any movement. Ordered to return to the southern side of the DMZ at 1400, started moving south. Air observer reported movement to the front. Stopped and deployed an ambush, killed an NVA machine gunner, returned to base on 410 by different route to avoid enemy. Alpha team made a home run along the river, made contact with a force of unknown size, was ordered to break contact and return by a different route. Later, the 27th of May, took 82 and 60mm mortar fire on the company position, with 8 wounded. Helicopter called in for medevac hit, crashed south of position, no kills. 28 May, company returned to Hill 290, where we are now. Hill 410 is now very bare, so you can see that in some of the pictures. Today is the 30th of May, Buddha's birthday, NVA declared a 48-hour truce, which has only been broken twice. It's getting dark now.

I'll send this tomorrow when the bird comes for some malaria medevacs. I'll also enclose some pictures. Don't really think this should go to Betsy. 10:00 o'clock 31 May 1969, we start moving at 0700 tomorrow toward the east, have been here for two days, the Buddha's birthday truce is still on. At home where you are, it's still yesterday so John (my brother) will be married here today, but there tomorrow. I think I understand that. I hope he's nervous. Please give him my best and pick out something nice for him and Pat for me and then bill me.

To answer your questions from the mail that came in yesterday, yes, I know that all the armed forces computers are screwed up. No, I don't know what to call him or her [our first child was about to be born] but sure am glad you both will be there for baptism. No, the United States Marine Corps promotes to 1st Lieutenant in 15-18 months, maybe. Job change uncertain. Don't think I'll get to stay with the platoon for much longer. Just requested an extension to stay with them for at least another two months. No answer yet. Will fill in details at some later time. My love to everyone. Please give my love and my very best to John and Pat.

3

INTO THE "Z"

LESS THAN AN HOUR HAD PASSED SINCE THE OPENING burst of enemy fire took Bill Haskell out of The War. But despite the loss of their Platoon Leader and five of their riflemen, the rapid response of his 1st Platoon and the furious follow-up attack by the 2d Platoon had driven the enemy back. Except for some occasional nervous firing at movement, real or imagined, by a few Marines, things were now relatively quiet. I began to think that the NVA, stunned by the air strikes and our assaults, had indeed broken contact and withdrawn.

Nevertheless, the men who called themselves "Blue's Bastards," the thirty-five remaining Marines of 2d Platoon, Company K, were very cautious as they began to move uphill. Before we passed

34

through the remnants of Haskell's 1st Platoon, Staff Sergeant Moncayo had redistributed ammunition among our men, some of it collected up from 1st Platoon's wounded. "Big Dan" Doan's 1st Squad took the lead and headed up the slope. Doc Swells, our 2d Platoon chief medical corpsman, Jim Lehnert, and I fell in at their rear. With Corporal Ervolina's 2d Squad on our left and Corporal Smith's 3d Squad on the right, the platoon formed a rough, inverted V, like a wedge, pointed up the hill. Within a few meters we passed the spot where Corporal Robert Dalton, one of Haskell's machine-gun team leaders, his M-60 weapon disabled by a piece of shrapnel, and carrying only his .45 pistol and some hand grenades, had organized a three-man assault on an NVA bunker. His action had broken the initial attack on 1st Platoon. Goodwin subsequently nominated him for the Navy Cross for his heroism.

As we edged up the hill, we passed two dozen or so NVA fighting positions, carefully dug and camouflaged to avoid detection from the air. The holes were connected by a well-concealed trench line that was invisible until we were practically standing over it. The complex looked big enough to have held 35 to 40 NVA soldiers. Inside the trenches and holes were hundreds of expended AK-47 and machine-gun cartridges, empty ammo boxes, several Claymore-type mines, "ChiCom" grenades, bloody bandages, and some broken weapons. Though we'd hurt them, they had still managed to drag off their dead and wounded, even as we were pounding them. Once again, I was amazed at their remarkable discipline.

For twenty or thirty minutes we moved very slowly and quietly up the slope. Often there was no sound at all except the distant thunder of the two Marine F-4 Phantoms, orbiting at high altitude, well to our south. We passed by their awesome handiwork, a series of deep, wide craters, the trees blown down by the terrible explosions or turned into stark stalks, blasted naked of foliage. Suddenly, Doan signaled a halt. His point man had spotted movement on the slope ahead. Every man, nerves already frayed from the earlier contact, crouched and peered into the thick vegetation.

Without waiting for me to turn and ask, Lehnert slipped the radio handset into my dirty, sweating palm. I called Goodwin and whispered into the mouthpiece that we had movement to our immediate front and that I wanted Lieutenant Art Vandaveer, the Artillery Forward Observer, to put a white phosphorous artillery round 200 meters in front of Doan's squad to mark the target and to have Sergeant Getze, the air spotter, tell the Phantoms to make another 500-pound-bomb run on the marking round.

For a change, everything worked just as it was supposed to—at least at first. Art crept forward and called in the artillery-fire mission. The "Willie Pete" hit right where it was aimed. The F-4s came rolling in, and the bombs dropped off their wings, right on target. And, as we'd practiced so many times, we were up and charging as soon as the hot breath of the second Phantom's bombs had blown past us.

It was textbook perfect except for one thing: The NVA were still there! And as soon as we moved, the air still heavy with the ammonia-like smell of the bombs' high explosives, the hillside in front of us erupted in a cascade of enemy rifle and machine-gun fire.

We were all immediately back on our bellies, and I grabbed at Lehnert's radio handset to call for another airstrike. And that's when things began to get very bad indeed. As the intensity of enemy fire picked up, Goodwin informed me that the two aircraft that had been supporting us were dangerously low on fuel and would have to head back to Da Nang. They promised to dispatch another two-plane "section" to help us but didn't know how long it would take. Goodwin had just delivered this delightful piece of news when a rocket-propelled grenade came whizzing past Lehnert and me and burst behind us.

I've heard other people describe moments like these. I've heard them say that "something just snapped" or that they "just went kind of crazy." I really don't recall it like that, nor do I really even know quite what caused my reaction. It could have been that RPG flying over our heads. It might have been seeing Haskell all shot to pieces. Maybe it was just that I had a very bad case of dysentery and all this shooting was keeping me from being able to do what my intestines wanted me to do.

Whatever it was, I remember getting angry, not losing my temper but just being very, very angry at this particular group of enemy soldiers. They had pinned us down and held us up long enough to withdraw to a second set of previously prepared positions, and they were now trying to do to Blue's

Bastards what they had done to Haskell's Rascals a little over an hour before.

I decided that if we couldn't drop bombs on them, we would put an artillery round on every step we had to take up this hill, no matter how long it took to get to the top. But before I could call in the next fire mission, a heavy machine gun opened up on us, and almost simultaneously, through the din we could hear the awful hiss of incoming mortar rounds. As they crashed among us, a fragment from one of the 60mm projectiles smashed into the back of Lehnert's radio, cutting off my call to Goodwin for mortar and artillery support. Worst of all, blood was running down Lehnert's sleeve, and he was grimacing in pain.

"Go! Get back down the hill, get Doc to look at that." I shouted at him in what he must have taken as anger.

"I'll be okay . . ." he started.

"Now, Jim! Go!"

He went.

I *was* angry. But not at him. Jim Lehnert had been my radio operator for more than six months and one of the most reliable people I've ever met. Rarely farther from me than the four-foot length of a radio handset cord, he carried on his back help when we needed it. The twenty-five-pound radio he "humped" was my link with Goodwin, my fellow platoon commanders, my own squad leaders, reinforcements, and supporting arms. But the way I felt about Jim Lehnert was based on more than just what he did and how well he did it. We had shared almost every waking moment, day and night, soaking cold in the monsoon and sweat-drenched in the sun, for what seemed an eternity. And we'd shared nearly everything else as well: food, water, news from home, anxieties, and hopes. Seeing him hurt made me even angrier.

With Lehnert gone, I needed a radio. We had to find some way of stopping the mortar fire or we would take so many casualties that an NVA counterattack down the hill could overrun our very precarious position. I made my way in short dashes between incoming mortar rounds to where 3d Squad was burrowing in for some protection from the incoming and came on Private First Class Wendell Thomas, a tough New Englander, who was carrying the squad's radio. Without hesitating, he, Private First Class Pete Markol, an M-79 grenadier, and two riflemen, Private First Class "Frenchie" Sirois, and Everett Whipple, joined me and we moved forward to join 1st Squad.

The five of us began the now familiar series of wind sprints to get up to where Doan and his men were pinned down. Halfway there, over ground that I was sure 1st Squad had already swept, an NVA soldier jumped out of one of those well-concealed fighting holes we had by now seen so many of, and raised his AK-47. We both fired at once.

The Marine issue Model 12 Winchester pump shotgun will forever be my favorite firearm. Loaded with military standard "00" buckshot, it is a lethal lifesaver at fifteen feet. The NVA soldier toppled over backward as I dove for the ground.

Before I could even contemplate the horror of what had just happened, two NVA "ChiCom" grenades came hurtling toward me, thrown by one of the dead soldier's comrades. One landed in front of me, the other behind. They went off split seconds apart. Had I still been standing, they surely would have killed me. As it was, I was peppered with tiny fragments from the blasts. I looked up to see the NVA soldier who had thrown them scurrying into the brush, raised up on one knee to fire, and found that I couldn't cock the shotgun. A metal fragment from one of the grenades had lodged in it. The pump action was jammed, and the weapon wouldn't work. I dropped it to the ground and drew my standard issue .45 pistol. But by now, the second NVA was out of sight.

There's no doubt that the shotgun had saved me. But if it hadn't been for Goodwin, I wouldn't even have had it. When he'd taken over as company commander, Goodwin had made me get rid of a very nice Swedish submachine gun that we'd captured in an ambush several months before he arrived. He said he didn't want his lieutenants "hot dogging it in some fire fight," and that "your job is to lead Marines, not play rifleman." He insisted that "if you want some kind of weapon besides your .45, I'll get you a shotgun."

What bugged us all about Goodwin was not that he was so often right, but that we knew he was even when we didn't want to admit it. As I left my now useless shotgun there in the dirt, I had to admit that he had been right again.

Sirois who had been directly behind me and unable to fire for fear of hitting me, came up and helped me put a couple of small battle dressings over the little holes in my right hand and leg while Whipple, Markol, and Thomas covered us. Then, exercising considerably more care than we had before, we crept up among Doan's 1st Squad, which had occupied another of the NVA trench lines. They were wisely using the enemy fortification as cover to shoot back at our tormentors.

As we tumbled into the trench, Thomas reestablished radio contact with the company command group. Directly behind us, 150 meters down the slope, Goodwin had set up a mini-aid station in one of the fresh bomb craters, a medevac LZ (landing zone) in another, and in a third, a mortar pit for our Company's 60mm mortars. I was trying to call in a fire mission for our 60s over the din of the firing when Lieutenant Art Vandaveer and Lance Corporal Johnson, his radio operator, crawled up beside me.

They brought with them eight men from 1st Platoon, carrying several boxes of machine-gun ammunition, three or four sandbags full of rounds for our M-79 grenade launchers, and a half dozen LAAWs, single-shot disposable rocket launchers. These particular weapons were designed for use against armored vehicles, but they were perfect for going against enemy emplacements like those in front of us.

On his way back to the company aid station, Lehnert had told Vandaveer of our plight and lack of communications, and the artillery lieutenant had decided to become a one-stop supermarket of munitions! The resupply of ammo was a godsend for the platoon. We quickly distributed it around to the men while Vandaveer plotted a fire mission. I asked him to mix in some "VT fuse," rounds that would burst in the air above the enemy trench line in front of us, and closer in, some more Willie Pete to obscure their vision.

Together—Vandaveer talking on his radio with the batteries of 105mm howitzers and 155mm guns at The Rockpile, and me on Thomas's radio with our company's 60mm mortars—we plotted a massive, "fire for effect," after which we would once again rush the enemy emplacements up the hill.

This time everything worked just as it should. As the mortar and artillery fire swept over the NVA positions, everyone in the platoon opened fire. For the third time in the afternoon, Blue's Bastards got up and assaulted the dug-in NVA. Once again the well-disciplined enemy withdrew in good order, and by the time we got to the positions they had occupied, we had four more wounded of our own and were too short of ammunition to continue the attack even though we were now only 100 meters or so from the top of the hill.

By now the fight had been going on for over three hours. The men were exhausted, terribly dehydrated, and again, dangerously short of ammunition. I passed the word to hold up, crouched down behind the trunk of an enormous tree that had been blown down in one of the air strikes, and got on the radio to Goodwin.

"We've got to get some more ammo up here. My guns [the M-60 machine guns] are down to one belt apiece. Nobody has more than one grenade left. Some have none. Let's hold up until we can get some more air [air strikes] on the hilltop and the area around it. I've got four more medevacs headed back down to the LZ. One or two of them need to get out right away if you can get another bird."

Goodwin listened, asked a few brief questions, and weighed it over. His terse response, "Roger, wait, out," meant that he was trying to measure the effects of postponing another attack. He knew that by delaying, we faced the very real possibility of not making it to the top of Hill 410 by nightfall and the terrible prospect of an NVA counterattack in the dark from the high ground above us. He also knew that we weren't the only ones with a precarious ammunition situation. The artillery batteries six miles south at The Rockpile were now running low, and our company 60mm mortars had fired so fast for so long that the tubes were red-hot. We were reduced to taking all but one magazine from the wounded before carrying them back down the hill. And the men were by now so weary that it was taking six of them to carry one wounded man the 250 meters back to the aid station and medevac LZ.

After our brief conversation, Goodwin conferred on the radio with the battalion commander, Lieutenant Colonel Dick Schulze, about two miles south, in the valley below us, then with the air- and artillery-support coordinators. All of this information went into Goodwin's decision.

When he came back on the radio four or five minutes later, he said, "Blue, hold where you are for right now. Keep calling in our 60's [the company's 60mm mortars] to keep 'em pinned down. Redistribute ammo as best you can. If we can't get more air support in a half an hour, we'll go with as much 'Arty' [artillery] as they'll give us. We've got to be on top of that hill before dark."

Goodwin's decision to postpone resuming the attack was a welcome relief. But waiting didn't mean resting. We were still taking fire, though much lighter than before. Despite the incredible number of artillery rounds Vandaveer had called in on the hilltop and the surrounding area, the tenacious NVA mortarmen were still able to lob three or four 60mm rounds at us every few minutes from somewhere north of the hilltop we were trying to reach. It seemed that given the amount they had already fired at us, they had to be shooting from the plant where they were made. To at least gain some protection from this lethal rain, the men who couldn't find space in an NVA hole or trench line, scraped shallow holes of their own with an entrenching tool in one hand and a weapon "at the ready" in the other.

The last assault had been so noisy that I hadn't heard the resupply and medevac helos coming and going from the little airport Goodwin had established in the bomb craters below us. He had used our attack as a diversion to slip four, twin-rotored, CH-46 resupply helicopters into the LZ. On their way out, they had medevacked most of our wounded.

Now, as we waited for more Marine, Navy, or Air Force planes to resume the bombing runs, the results of the emergency resupply Goodwin had conjured up became evident. The Company Gunnery Sergeant, John Banta, organized a human conveyor belt behind us, and Marines from 1st and

3d Platoons handed, from man-to-man up the hill, boxes of ammunition, crates of grenades, LAAWs, and belts of machine-gun ammo that had been lowered in nets by the helos. They also passed up to us, though they too were parched with thirst, five-gallon plastic water containers that we handed up and down the line so that long-empty canteens could be replenished.

Because the men were so bone tired, the distribution of ammunition and water took longer than it should have, but it also gave Lieutenant Vandaveer and Sergeant Getze the time to carefully plan the artillery fires and air strikes for our final assault. From the relative safety of a well-constructed NVA bunker, we worked out essential coordination to avoid an unpleasant collision, high in the air above us, of a friendly U.S. Marine jet and a friendly U.S. Marine artillery round. Those are the kinds of things that pilots get upset about, and we certainly didn't want them mad at us today.

As the synchronized air and artillery strikes began, Staff Sergeant Moncayo and I placed into the line the Marines from 1st and 3d Platoon who had been ferrying supplies up the hill. With them came Lehnert with a replacement radio, his injury less serious than I'd thought. I was overjoyed to have him back.

The accuracy and volume of our fire suppressed the NVA's weapons and made it safer to move about, giving the squad leaders a last chance to encourage their spent Marines to one final effort. The final assault over the top of the hill was an extraordinary example of what brave men can do despite absolute exhaustion. Not one of those filthy, sweat-drenched, totally drained men wanted to get back up and charge into the miniature hell on top of that hill. But they did.

And in spite of the exhilaration of succeeding in a terribly difficult task, no one, when we finally occupied the bunker complex on the scarred and smoking crest, felt any euphoria. It was now almost 5:30 and the sun was beginning to set. The fight to get "Kilo" Company to the top of this hill on the edge of the DMZ had taken over four hours and cost twelve wounded Marines. Some, Bill Haskell among them, were very seriously hurt and would be sent home from The War.

We staggered through blasted trees and bomb craters to establish a rough perimeter on what had been an NVA base. From the north side of the slope we could look across the Ben Hai River into their homeland. To the west, 1st Squad was still firing at movement down the side of the hill as the NVA withdrew. We hadn't yet swept the area for enemy wounded or stragglers when I saw Goodwin approaching. I was sitting, exhausted, on the trunk of a downed tree, holding my pistol. I noticed that he, too, had his .45 out, but in his other hand he had the disabled shotgun I had discarded hours before.

"How many more casualties?" he asked.

"Two more, I think, but I don't have a full report from 2d squad yet. We've got a lot of 1st and 3d Platoon mixed in with our people. We'll have it all straightened out in a few minutes," I replied.

"Do you have OPs [Observation Posts] out to the north yet?"

"Not yet, but Staff Sergeant Moncayo is seeing to it as soon as we get a head count and match it up with the medevac roster." I didn't even want to think about an MIA or the possibility that one of our people had been taken prisoner by the retreating NVA.

"Good," he said. Then, after a pause he pointed to the bandage on my hand and the dried blood on my right leg and asked, "How bad is it?"

"Not bad, a couple of little pieces from a grenade," I replied.

He was silent for a while, surveying the blasted rubble of what had once been a quiet, jungle-covered hill. When Goodwin looked back at me, shaking his head, he said, "Lieutenant, you sure do make a messy battlefield."

I looked at him, not sure if he was joking or serious, but I could see the beginning of a smile through the sweat-caked grime that covered his face.

"And by the way, Lieutenant, what's the idea disposing of this shotgun? You do realize that this is U.S. Government property, don't you?"

"Yes, sir, I do, but you see, it's no good anymore. There is a grenade fragment in the slide, and it can't be cocked."

"What do you mean it's no good anymore? It's still a perfectly good club."

Goodwin couldn't have been too upset at the "messy battlefield" or at my turning the shotgun he'd gotten me into a "perfectly good club." In the days that followed he put me in for the Silver Star and wrote glowing words that appear on the citation for "conspicuous gallantry and intrepidity in action" that came with the medal. But the words about that battle that mean the most to me aren't on that yellowed sheet of paper in my footlocker. The best thing said about me in that fight and perhaps in the twenty-two years I spent in the Marines, were spoken by Private First Class Frenchie Sirois, when he and a small group of Blue's Bastards came up to Goodwin and me on that hilltop.

Frenchie Sirois, was a Canadian and we used to kid him about being sent to America to join the U.S. Marines as restitution for all the draft dodgers who had fled to Canada. But Frenchie was also a very courageous man and he, Everett Whipple, Pete Markol, and Wendell Thomas had stayed with me for most of the fight up to the top of Hill 410. They had fought, crawled, and scrambled their way from position to position, distributing ammo, passing out water, and encouraging their desperately fatigued comrades. Everywhere I turned, at least one of them would be there—ready, protecting. I had, in the course of that long afternoon, developed enormous admiration for these brave men, though there were times when I was sure that they were following me because they had made a bet on how and when the lieutenant would "get it."

Now the four of them were standing in front of Goodwin. Frenchie spoke: "Captain, you should have seen my lieutenant. He was magnificent."

It wasn't the word *magnificent* that meant so much. It was what he called me—not "the lieutenant," or "Blue," or "Lieutenant North," but "*my* lieutenant."

To this day those words mean more to me than everything else said or written about my time in the Marines. The very brave young men of 2d Platoon, Company K weren't mine—I was *theirs*! They called themselves Blue's Bastards, but they didn't belong to me. I was blessed to be one of *them* .

4

WINNING WAS NOT OUR MISSION

Vietnam: 8 March 1965

WHEN THE FIRST U.S. COMBAT FORCES ARRIVED IN Vietnam at a little after 9:00 A.M. on the 8th of March, 1965, no one could have imagined that more than four years later, units like mine would still be in Vietnam, much less on the edge of the DMZ. In fact, many of those who participated in the initial landing in 1965 believed their arrival to be a prelude to the end of the insurgency that threatened the freedom of South Vietnam. Certainly the reception that Battalion Landing Team 3/9, of the 3d Marine Division, received that morning would have led anyone to believe that America's military involvement in Vietnam wasn't going to last very long.

When the Marines of BLT 3/9 touched down

on "Red Beach" just north of the port city of Da Nang, they were loaded for war, each man weighed down by 70 – 80 pounds of gear. They were not met, however, by enemy guns but by news cameras and beautiful girls in white silk *ao dais* bearing flowers.

Despite the lovely greeting when they arrived, for the next six years, Marine units would conduct combat operations in the northern quarter of this near-mystical land. But few other encounters with the local population were as pleasant as the welcome received that sunlit spring morning in 1965.

When that first Vietnam landing occurred, I was a midshipman at the U.S. Naval Academy in Annapolis, Maryland. One of the upper-class midshipmen in my company who knew I was going into the Marines when I graduated, ordered me to the company wardroom to watch TV news footage of the Marine Corps entry into Vietnam and to chide me for the Corps' unnecessarily warlike landing. Nearly twenty-eight years later, another Marine BLT made a similar landing on a beach in Somalia. Like the one in Vietnam, I saw the Marine landing in Somalia on television and read about it in the newspaper. And as they did in Vietnam in 1965, the press covering of the Somalia landing made light of the Marines' readiness for combat.

Though no one today claims credit for envisioning it at the time, the single reinforced infantry battalion of fewer than 2,500 Marines that landed in Vietnam in March of 1965 would eventually grow to more than two full Marine divisions, two air wings, and their associated Combat Support and Service Support units. By the time I arrived "in country" at the war's peak in 1968, more than 88,000 Marines were serving in Vietnam. The area assigned to the Marines had gradually increased from a portion of a single airfield to an area of more than 10,000 square miles, officially known as I Corps Tactical Zone.

The U.S. military hierarchy in Saigon, at Pacific Command in Hawaii, and the brass back in Washington abbreviated the name for this northernmost of the four military regions of South Vietnam as "ICTZ." The officers who served there called it "I Corps." Most of the troops simply called it "Nam." For nearly all, it had the ingredients for a special kind of hell.

The area included the Republic of Vietnam's five northernmost provinces: Quang Tri, Thua Thien, Quang Nam, Quang Tin, and Quang Nghai. It stretched 225 miles from the DMZ, south to the beginning of the central highlands. Bordered by the South China Sea to the east and Laos on the west, the region was as little as thirty miles deep and no more than seventy miles at its widest point.

Except for the Hai Van mountains, which tumble directly into the sea north of Da Nang, I Corps was fairly consistent in its terrain. The coastal plains edge gradually upward to the west, the piedmont becoming steeper and more precipitous the closer one gets to Laos.

Along Vietnam's western border are some of the highest and steepest mountains in Southeast Asia. These mist-shrouded, jungle-covered slopes run nearly the full length of South Vietnam. It is some of the most beautiful—and deadly—terrain that Americans have ever fought in. It was here that the experts in Washington decided that the Marine Corps should come in 1965.

That spring in Washington, as planners at the Pentagon and the White House began to piecemeal units into this faraway land, no one realized that the fight we were entering would last more than half a decade. Nor did they envision that the war would eventually cost the lives of more than 58,000 Americans. Certainly, as BLT 3/9 crossed Red Beach, no one could have imagined that we were embarking on a catastrophic defeat and nearly two decades of bitter recriminations.

The Marines of BLT 3/9 were not the first U.S. personnel to arrive "in country." A handful of U.S. Army, Navy, Air Force, and Marine advisors had served in Vietnam since the country was partitioned following the French defeat in 1954. In 1962 President Kennedy ordered U.S. Marine helicopter squadrons to Da Nang to support South Vietnamese efforts to deal with the growing Viet Cong insurgency. In 1964 President Johnson sent U.S. Air Force fighter and attack squadrons to Da Nang and further south to Ton Son Nhut and Bien Hoa. By March of 1965 the Marine contingent at the Da Nang Airbase included a HAWK anti-aircraft missile battalion and totaled nearly 1,300 men.

By the time I got to Vietnam in November 1968 there were a good number of officers and senior enlisted who were returning for second tours of duty. They hadn't all volunteered for another stint in Vietnam. Many had just stayed in the service long enough that their numbers came up again.

When they got there for their second tour in 1968 or 1969, they found a different war and different warriors than they had served with just a few short years before. Those who came to "the Nam" with those first U.S. Army and Marine battalions had arrived and departed as whole units—as did BLT 3/9 on Red Beach. But by the time I got there, the rotation of units that had been assembled, trained, and deployed together had been scrapped and supplanted with individual replacements on thirteen-month, and later, twelve-month, assignments. Unit Deployment, the concept that had brought victory in World War II, had been deemed to be too costly. But we had fought WWII to win. Though few of us on the ground knew it at the time, winning wasn't our mission in Vietnam.

For the "green eyeshade" military analysts and management experts in the Pentagon, cost wasn't the only factor. They also claimed that the "learning curve" for fresh units arriving in country was too long. They could show, statistically, a reduction in combat effectiveness while units fresh from the U.S. or Okinawa became acclimated to the heat and humidity and gained familiarity with the terrain and the enemy. Of course, "combat effectiveness" was all a matter of "kill ratios."

For the McNamara-era military personnel managers in Washington's air-conditioned offices, the concept of individual, one-year "tours" made great sense. For those of us in the field it was a disaster.

To troops in combat, unit cohesion is as important as good tactics and equipment. Knowing and trusting those on your right and left is an essential ingredient on every team. In combat, where the stakes of the game are life and death, it is critical. And yet from 1968 onward, nearly every combat unit was caught in a virtual tornado of constant personnel turbulence.

I can't imagine a football team's substituting three or four completely new players into the line-up for each play when the only thing the team captain or coach knows about the new players is the positions they are to play and the numbers on their backs. But that's what it was like for those of us who tried to fight in Vietnam. A helicopter would land, two or three of your most experienced troops would get on and disappear, and their replacements—often a rank or two lower and far less experienced than those who left—would arrive on another helo a day or two later. Often, the replacements would be evacuated from wounds, sickness, or worse before we even got to know them.

All of these factors, and of course the war's final outcome, combined to shape the way Vietnam is remembered by those who lived through it—whether they fought in it or not. Our nation was deeply wounded by the "Vietnam experience." Perhaps the only parallel in our history is the American South after the Civil War. But in the modern era, there is nothing that compares to the anger, frustration, and sadness that persists from the only war we ever lost.

The veterans of Vietnam did not come home as national heroes like those who fought in World Wars I and II, or even Korea. There were no victory parades. Our return was heralded privately by families and loved ones, marked more by personal sighs of great relief than acts of patriotic celebration.

By the time I served in Vietnam, from the end of 1968 through 1969, few really wanted to be there and fewer still were those who looked forward to going back. But by then, those of us who stayed in the service also expected that the time would come when we would get orders for Vietnam again.

Sometimes the demand for those with "Vietnam experience" was much greater than the supply. Shortages of aviators assured pilots, particularly those who flew helicopters, a swift return to combat duty after just a short tour back in the United States. For me, it was much easier. After my tour in "the Nam," I was assigned for a three year tour at Quantico, Virginia, training new officers who, in many cases, were on their way to the war I had come from. Until 1993, my only trip back to Vietnam was in 1970, when I returned briefly to testify at a court martial on behalf of one of the Marines who had served with me in Blue's Bastards.

When our battalion departed Vietnam at the end of 1969, Marines who had more than six months remaining on their year-long tour were reassigned to units in the 1st Marine Division. Randy Herrod had been a machine-gun team leader with my rifle platoon, and he fit into this category. During a fierce nighttime battle in July 1969, Herrod had, almost singlehandedly, beat off an NVA attack against our perimeter. During the engagement he also saved my life. Afterward he was awarded the Silver Star.

When 3/3 left for Okinawa, Herrod was sent south to Da Nang and assigned to the 1st Marine Division. There he found a different war and a different adversary. Where we had been fighting main force NVA units and rarely if ever saw a civilian, he was now confronted with Viet Cong, very often intermingled with civilians. One night the ambush patrol he was leading opened fire on what they believed to be Viet Cong guerrillas. Some of them were, but there were also civilians killed. He was promptly brought before a court martial.

When I heard about the incident, I asked for permission to fly back to Vietnam to testify at his trial. Thankfully, he was vindicated. That was August 1970.

Though there were some who volunteered to go back after their initial twelve- or thirteen-month tour, there were very few people who truly wanted to return. While I was certainly willing to go back to Vietnam if so ordered, I wasn't about to go back any earlier than I had to.

First, Betsy and I were starting a family. By 1971 we had two small children and were talking about a third. I know some people have trouble thinking of Marines being husbands and fathers, but many of us are and we have as much fun at it as our civilian counterparts. I also had other reservations. By 1971, it was very clear to me that the politicians in Washington had decided that we were going to fight a war but then chose not to win it. Early on, before I'd ever gotten to Vietnam, they had created conditions that made victory impossible.

At Annapolis I had been a boxer, and in 1967 I won the Naval Academy Boxing Championship in my weight class. It seemed to me that by 1970 what we were being asked to do in Vietnam was about the same as if Emerson Smith, my boxing coach, had asked me to get in the ring and throw the fight. I knew he wouldn't do such a thing, and

I couldn't understand how our political leaders could ask those of us in uniform to do it when the stakes were so high.

No warrior, no matter how motivated, wants to be told to fight but not to win. That's what we felt was happening in Vietnam in 1970.

5

THE TALK OF WAR

ONE OF THE THINGS I MOST REMEMBER ABOUT combat is that most of it isn't. I mean most of it isn't combat, fighting, being shelled, seeing people killed. Someone once described war as ninety-nine percent boredom and one percent stark terror. That's not far off the mark.

You spend most of your time getting ready to kill someone—and hoping that you won't be killed yourself. In that process you spend countless hours with people you otherwise would never have met in life—and discussing with them some of the most mundane and intimate things in the world.

In the nearly seven months that Jim Lehnert was my radio operator, I probably had more conversations with him than I did with my wife and best friend, Betsy, over the next three years, simply because Jim and I were *always* together. Unfortunately, Betsy and I were not.

During long, cold, wet nights, and steamy, sweaty days under a white-hot sun I came to know Jim Lehnert better than I had known my own brothers and sister.

We spent hours in detailed conversation about everything from cars, to our families, to the quality (or lack of it) of our equipment. I remember a lengthy conversation one night about the way our boots were put together, what was wrong with them, and how we could make them better.

In small groups these conversations—almost always in hushed tones, sometimes superficial, sometimes deeply philosophical—could go on for hours, even days. Sometimes they would even be reconvened after having been punctuated by some horrible event like a firefight, incoming NVA mortar or artillery rounds, or a nighttime probe of our position.

When I was a kid we played Monopoly. In the summer a Monopoly game could go on for a week—punctuated by meals, sleep, a trip to the neighborhood pool. These conversations were very much like those youthful board games.

With Goodwin and the other officers and the senior enlisted men it was the same. Waiting was an opportunity, once the business at hand was dispatched, to talk about something, anything, that had little or nothing to do with the war. It was an escape from the reality and horror of it all.

Very few of these conversations dealt with the enemy, or the dead, or the horribly wounded. Mostly those thoughts were kept to oneself because they hurt too much to express them openly. And after all, Marines don't cry—where others can see.

After I returned from the war, when I began to see the problems of racial friction that developed here in the States and at our overseas bases, it struck me that much of this kind of problem never arose in combat because of those long talks. Regardless of background, prior experiences, or educational differences, we came to know each other with an intimacy that some were never to replicate. I would venture to say that some of us shared more deeply on the battlefield than we ever did with those we loved at home.

I've often thought that Harry Truman must have had the nation's future in mind when he directed the integration of the U.S. Armed Forces in 1947. It was the real start of integration in this country—and made possible the legislation passed later under Presidents Eisenhower and Johnson.

The men who went home from the Korean War, who had served in integrated units, on integrated ships, and in integrated squadrons, learned that a man puts his pants on the same way no matter what color his skin may be. They learned about life on both sides of the color barrier in war's stinking holes and foul trenches and freezing cold. They came home and voted and ran for office, and some became legislators who, because of their wartime experiences, knew in their hearts that segregation was wrong.

Harry won't get the credit—but he deserves it—for making possible all those long, seemingly pointless conversations among men of different cultures and colors by which we all learned that most of us—regardless of our backgrounds—all have the same hopes, and dreams and aspirations.

It was a vital lesson because within days of arriving in Vietnam we all learned that men also all die the same way, no matter where they come from, no matter what language they speak, no matter what color they are.

I hope that America's sons and daughters never have to go to war again, especially a war like Vietnam. But at the same time, I wish they would be forced to spend hour after hour talking just above a whisper in a foxhole. Better yet, try it with Bill Clinton and Rush Limbaugh, Ross Perot and Jesse Jackson, Pat Robertson and Ted Kennedy.

Something tells me that if they were forced to spend a weekend together in one big muddy trench, with machine-gun bullets whizzing overhead, they'd find a way to solve a lot of problems.

6

HOW WAR FEELS

CERTAIN MEMORIES OF VIETNAM I SHALL NEVER forget. Some I can still almost feel:

How within seconds of standing up with 70 – 80 pounds strapped on your back, a helmet, flak jacket, weapon, grenades, extra ammo, an entrenching tool, your food and water, a first-aid pack, and the accumulated letters from home, you begin to sweat. And then, as the sun burns through the morning mist, it really starts getting hot.

How quietly hundreds of men carrying thousands of pounds of equipment can move when their lives depend on it.

Sunlight so intense, so hot, that it had to be carried like an extra weight on your back.

The incredible strain of trying to carry and balance a load while climbing up a hill with sweat running down into your eyes from underneath your helmet and knowing that if you lose your concentration just one split second you may have missed the chance to save your life and those of your comrades.

The incredible flying, crawling, slithering, stinging, biting, chewing, blood sucking insects, bugs, slugs, leeches, and varmints of Vietnam that had to have been bred in some Russian laboratory.

The obscene hiss of an incoming mortar round that gives the lie to that old axiom that "you never hear the one that gets you."

The boot-sucking mud that added ten pounds to each foot, every step you took.

The call of a rock ape and the roar of tigers on some forlorn mountaintop, mocking our presence and engines of war.

The extraordinary beauty of a land that could be incredibly deadly to all forms of humanity.

The mind-numbing boredom of walking up and down those endless hills following the green-clad, sweat-soaked back of the Marine in front of you and knowing that everyone in that little unit hopes and prays that you know what you are doing and where you are going and that you will somehow get them home from this terrible experience—alive and in one piece.

The adrenaline rush and gut-wrenching nausea that happen in those moments of sheer terror that punctuated the boredom.

The horrible scream, like the cry of an animal, when one of your men is hit.

The smell of blood spilled in quantities so great that it turns the soil black.

The terrible smallness you feel when your prayer is not answered in a way that can be understood, and the man you hold in your arms shudders and dies.

7

DEATH IN THE DARKNESS

Vietnam: July 1969

SOME NIGHTS WERE WORSE THAN OTHERS, BUT THE night that Private First Class Frank Coulombe and Captain Mike Wunsch were killed was the worst of all. A little after 2:30 in the morning, sitting in the cupola on top of his tank's turret, peering through a starlight scope, the Captain thought he detected enemy movement outside our perimeter. He radioed, asking me to join him on top of the tank so that I could see what he had seen—to confirm his suspicion.

I came immediately. My platoon was interspersed among the steel behemoths of his tank company and Captain Mike Wunsch was a man I very much admired and respected—and not just because he, like me, was a Naval Academy graduate. He was immensely liked by his men, and he had taught them well how to work with infantry. His was one of the few Marine armor units that would willingly stay out in "the bush" at night. Most "tankers" preferred to bring their expensive, noisy, armor-plated monsters into a fixed base when the sun went down. But not Mike Wunsch. Here he was, with two platoons of his tank company, thirteen tanks in all, seven kilometers southwest of Con Thien Base Camp. Earlier in the day he had told me that he wanted to go with us because he would be rotating home in a matter of days and he wanted one last mission with his men before departing.

I climbed up on the tank and stood beside him to look through the night-vision scope and realized instantly what had happened. A large group of NVA soldiers were approaching up the north side of the draw, opposite my listening post. My men thought that they had heard movement but saw nothing. I needed to immediately alert our listening posts and the rest of the perimeter. Several NVA were fewer than fifty meters in front of us, and there were undoubtedly more behind them.

I turned to get off the back of the tank and had taken only a single step in the dark when an RPG round struck the front of the tank's cupola. It deflected off the curved armor and detonated, killing Captain Wunsch instantly—and blowing me off the back of the tank.

If I had waited a second more, the same rocket would have killed me, for I had been standing right next to him just an instant before. As it was, the blast threw me about ten feet behind the tank, shredding the back of my flak jacket and peppering the back of my legs, buttocks, and neck with fragments. Even my ears had little pinholes through them.

I awoke what must have been moments later, being dragged toward a hole on the edge of the perimeter. Randy Herrod, my machine-gun team leader in the position to the left of the captain's tank had rushed out from the protection of his hole to drag me to safety.

Despite the noise of explosions all around me, every sound was muffled. My eardrums, just healed from the battle on May 25, had been blown out again.

Herrod threw me into the bottom of his fighting hole and stood on top of me firing his machine gun as the NVA swept up the side of the hill behind a barrage of mortar fire and a hail of RPGs. I remember trying to push him off me so I could get out of the hole and to my radio, an effort that succeeded only because Randy had to scramble out of his position to remount his M-60 machine gun, which had been blown off its mount by an exploding grenade or RPG.

Despite the chaos it was clear that the full force of the attack was imminent because the rain of enemy mortar fire was now shifting to the far side of our little perimeter.

The air was so thick with enemy fire, much of it unanswered, that even the grass around the tanks was being cut down. Two tanks were now ablaze, lighting up our position, and silhouetting the infantry positions beside them. The west side of the perimeter would have to be reinforced or they would be inside and among us. Herrod's machine gun was all that was keeping them from breaking through.

Once out of the hole, I dashed to the back of the command tank. The radio I had placed there when I'd climbed up to look through Captain Wunsch's starlight scope was a shattered wreck visible in the light of the flares now raining over our heads. I sprinted to the next tank and got on the infantry phone at the tank's rear. The tank commander immediately rotated his turret, adjusted his fire across our front, and mowed down the first wave of the oncoming assault.

There was a sudden lull in the enemy's attack. The brutal carnage produced by the tank's volley had a stunning effect. The NVA fell back, then regrouped and fired another volley of their own—more mortars and RPGs. They were so close that their rounds had to have caused casualties among their own men. One of the incoming rounds landed beside me. It blew me into the air, and once again I landed behind Herrod's hole.

For the second time in less than half an hour, Herrod left the relative protection of his fighting position, grabbed me by the remnants of my flak jacket, and dragged me to safety.

The second attack broke off under fire from Herrod's machine gun and the tanks on the west side of the perimeter. Once again I crawled out of the hole, found Jim Lehnert and a working radio, and started trying to adjust the air support that Goodwin had summoned on his radio from the company command post he'd set up in a bomb crater near the center of the perimeter. Because I couldn't hear, Lehnert passed the instructions to the AC-130s and shouted to me what the pilots were saying as they rained death from the heavens to break the third and final attack of the night.

Before dawn it was over.

The line had held, but the slaughter was awful. The tankers, restricted to a fixed perimeter, had fared worse than the infantry—suffering most of our seventeen killed and wounded. In the first light of dawn we found Private First Class Frank Coulombe's body. He had been killed by a burst of fire from an AK-47. His teammate on the listening post, though unconscious and badly wounded, was medevacked by helicopter to the hospital ship off shore.

For the NVA it was far worse. Despite the ferocity of their assault, only a handful had survived the three waves of attacks. Before he died, Captain Wunsch had deployed his tanks well. In doing so he saved the rest of us. The NVA had died in heaps as the fléchette rounds from his armor and the grazing fire of the machine guns cut them down in rows. One NVA soldier had been crushed under the treads of a tank as it adjusted its position. Among their dead were two officers.

Before the sun rose over the battlefield, the North Vietnamese survivors had melted away into the jungle to die elsewhere, to be buried in unmarked graves, or to fight again.

Shortly after first light the helicopters began their gruesome, flapping treks—evacuating first the wounded, then the dead, and delivering more ammunition for the next battle.

We stacked the weapons of the dead—AK-47s and RPGs from the enemy, M-16s from the

Marines—in the nets the ammo was delivered in. They were flown out last.

Before the victors left that hill, undamaged tanks towing those that could not move themselves, we buried the enemy's dead. We placed thermite grenades in the two tanks that were too damaged to move and abandoned them forever to rust and the elements. Then we moved on.

8

FACING LIFE AND MAKING CHOICES

WHY WAS MIKE WUNSCH KILLED AND NOT I? WHY did Bill Haskell have the point that day on the way to Hill 410? Why do some people get hurt or killed, and not others?

For anyone raised in America it ought to be pretty easy to choose between right and wrong. I suppose it's sometimes harder for people to make the choices between good and better: Are you going to buy a Ford or a Chevy? But life's toughest choices are between bad and worse.

If I didn't already know it before the battle where Bill Haskell was injured, I certainly knew afterward that we are sometimes presented with situations in which we have to make very difficult choices—and the only options are bad and worse. There are times in combat when you simply have to get people up and get them moving or more people are going to get hurt simply by staying where they are. In the chaos, noise, and pandemonium of battle, people often have to make those kinds of very difficult decisions. That's what officers and senior enlisted, noncommissioned officers get paid to do. More often than not those decisions—between bad and worse—have to be made with incomplete, sometimes conflicting information. And while the persons called upon to make these kinds of decisions may well know the outcome they hope to achieve, they usually know that it is more likely to be an outcome that is completely unexpected. In other words, combat leaders *must* make tough decisions whether or not they know what will happen next. Vietnam taught me those lessons, and I've taken them with me through the rest of life.

I suppose we are all, at various points in our lives, confronted by choices that are either bad or worse when we *have* to do something. I know some officers who, to this day, look back in anguish and say things like, "If I'd only called in one more air strike," or, "If we had just prepped the hill a little bit longer," or, "If we'd sent a squad farther around to one side, maybe we would have taken fewer casualties."

It is possible, I suppose, for a person to second-guess himself to the grave. But I don't think that's the way people are supposed to live. We're all going to make mistakes. That's because we're all frail, flawed mortals. Nothing is going to change that.

When I was teaching young lieutenants at Quantico after I got back from Vietnam, I used to try to give them some of this philosophy:

"Prepare for the worst, hope for the best, and settle for something in between"; or,

"Doing nothing won't help. You're better off doing something wrong than nothing at all"; and,

"If you make a mistake, trying the best you can, get back up and press on. Just don't make the same mistake twice."

I don't know whether these little pearls of wisdom helped the new lieutenants or not, but they sure have helped me over the years in coping with the realities of life.

Many people, vets included, are constantly trying to figure out why certain events turned out the way they did. I can think of scores of cases where it could have, maybe even should have, been different from what actually occurred.

Betsy puts it best when she says, "When I get to heaven, I've got a lot of questions I'd like to have answered. But between now and then, it's His plan, and I don't have to understand it all."

9

THE PRESERVATION OF INNOCENCE

WHILE RUMMAGING THROUGH SOME OLD NOTES and clippings, I discovered a flimsy, yellowed military telegram—a "cable"—from Vietnam. Though badly faded, most of the arcane abbreviations and acronyms, the jargon of military communicators, could still be read:

O P 130822Z JUN 69
FM CG THIRD MARDIV (REIN)
TO RUEBHOA/CMC
INFO RUEBOIA/BUMED
RHMSMVHA/COMUSMACV
RHMMAFA/CG FMFMPAC
RHMMAFA/CG III MAF
ZEN/THIRD BN THIRD MAR
BT
UNCLAS E F T O

REPORT OF CASUALTIES (1019 – 69)
A. MCO 3040.3C
B. FMFPACO P3040.2D
1. IAW REF A AND B FOL INFO IS SUB:
  TOTAL
NO OF CAS THIS RPT
TEN (10) HOSTILE AND FOUR (4) NON-
  HOSTILE.

In cryptic military prose, the 3d Marine Division was simply making its 1019th report of casualties in 1969 back to "the world." The message coolly recounted the status of the fourteen Marines from Northern "I Corps" who were listed as casualties on this report. Two-thirds of the way down the page is the fuzzy notation: :

(11) 2NDLT OLIVER L. NORTH 010 61
52/0302 USMC, CO K, 3/3, 3D MARDIV,
WIANE 25MAY69, VICINITY DMZ, APRX 6
MI NW OF CAM LO, QUANG TRI PROVINCE,
RVN. RECD FRAGWD RIGHT HAND, RIGHT
LEG FR EN GRENADE WHILE ENGAGED IN
ACT AGNST HOSTILE FOR DUR OP VIR-
GINIA RIDGE. CONDITION AND PROGNO-
SIS GOOD. LOC AT BAS, QUANG TRI. REQR
TRMT BY DOCTOR. REQ NOK NOT BE
NOTIFIED. PH TO BE AWD.

For each of the thirteen other entries on that same report there is a rank, a name, a serial number, branch of service, unit to which assigned, the date and type of injury, where it happened, and how. Nearly all had a final notation that, translated into English, said: "Request that next of kin not be notified. Purple Heart to be awarded."

Why did so many of us who got hurt or wounded or sick want our families, those who loved us best, not to know what had happened? In many cases it was probably for the same reason that I didn't want Betsy or my parents notified: I didn't want them to worry. I hadn't been seriously injured, and I'd only been medevacked because days after it happened, the fragment punctures in my hand and leg became badly infected.

But that clearly wasn't always the case. Others who were terribly sick with malaria, strange tropical diseases, or who were suffering from serious, even disfiguring wounds and injuries did the same.

In the text of that message from June of 1969 that reported my rather superficial wounds, there is the account of a Marine corporal from 3d Battalion, 9th Marines, who was recuperating on one of the Navy's hospital ships from the severe burns and eye injuries he had suffered when a helicopter was hit by enemy fire, crashed, and exploded. His certainly weren't minor wounds, yet the report of his injuries included the notation:

REQ NOK NOT BE NOTIFIED.
PH TO BE AWD.

In looking at these narratives today, I can see that many of us made a major error in trying to hide the horror of what was happening from those who loved and missed us. It also reflected a certain denial in all of us that things were as serious as they were. Worst of all, it contributed to a certain level of distrust between the veteran when he returned and those who had waited in uncertainty at home, for when they saw us for the first time in uniform, the medals told the story that we had not shared with them in our absence. They almost begged the question of anxious wives and parents who had waited prayerfully: "If he didn't tell us about the wounds, what other horror is he hiding?" Throughout my year-long tour, I wrote to Betsy regularly, but the letters were never chronicles of battle.

Looking back at them now, I see upbeat descriptions of people and places, graphic descriptions of how much I missed her, and lengthy recitations of the affection I felt for her. They were all true and accurate as far as they went, but they never told the whole story. Somehow, I naïvely assumed that she shouldn't be burdened with the rest of it. It took her a long time for her to forgive me for not having shared it with her.

The letters I penned to my dad were more specific. Twenty-five years before, he, too, had served in combat as an infantry officer. In World War II he had faced the harsh, life-or-death realities of the European theater. He knew the hard choices that sometimes have to be made in combat, knew about pain and sweat, deadly fatigue and endless boredom, and the real meaning of absolute, stark terror.

Those were things that had gone through my mind when I wrote the explicit, descriptive letters to Dad and very different ones to Betsy. I reasoned, incorrectly, that sharing the experiences and concerns of a young officer would not cause him the same fear and anguish that it might an innocent, young wife. Today, a quarter of a century older and perhaps a little wiser, I can look back and see that it was a mistake not to have shared more of my fears, anxieties, and apprehension with Betsy. She was, after all, and is, the person with whom I chose to spend the rest of my life.

But these words are written after more than two decades of living with her, coming to know her better, and to love her even more. They are also written fifteen years after we both came to have a deeply personal relationship with our Lord and Savior. Those experiences we have shared have allowed us to be more open with each other than when I was writing to her from Vietnam.

But even with our shared, life-changing experiences, there are still things about Vietnam that Betsy cannot grasp today because she was not there and because I failed to articulate them at the time. For example, she does not fully understand the affection I feel for Jim Lehnert, my radio operator for more than half a year in hell.

And it is precisely because it was hell that I and many others who served in Vietnam choose to keep from those we love most our worst horrors. It is one thing to share the concerns and anxieties of life with a helpmate, even though that loved one may not fully understand. It is quite another to subject them to the same experience.

Everyone should be spared the horrifying trauma of war. Having experienced it myself, and having witnessed firsthand its effects on the women and children of Vietnam, I cannot help but question the wisdom of some of our politicians who want women to serve in combat. All wars are not like

Desert Storm—over in a hundred hours. Vietnam was week after week of hundred-hour wars, at least fifty-two of them for most who served there. And for those who want a more modern example, ask any woman who has lived through the horror of Bosnia, Croatia, or Serbia, how she feels about women's serving in combat.

Wars are rarely as sanitary and swift as the Gulf War. Most have been and still will be brutal, bloody, and back-breaking. But even the most high-tech war, with laser-guided missiles and so-called smart-bombs, wrenches life from innocents. And brave young warriors are cut down in the blink of an eye. I hope my son, Stuart, never has to experience war.

I don't want him to have to go through what I experienced. No decent man wishes the experience of war for his son, much less for his wife and daughters.

Betsy's family has roots deeply planted in the soil of the American South. Her most famous recent ancestor was JEB Stuart, the Confederate cavalry officer. In the Civil War that rent this nation, the women and children of the southern states suffered, much as those in Vietnam did. In the 1860s, Betsy's family lived in what was then a battle zone. Today, we live in the Shenandoah Valley of Virginia, less than a mile from where blood was spilled in battle. Thankfully, most Americans never have to think of such terrible things.

We have been blessed, by God's providence and geography, not to have suffered war on our own soil in our lifetimes, but the horrifying images of what happened in the Republic of Vietnam, or

Yugoslavia, could well have been recorded in our own land a hundred thirty years ago: homes burned to the ground; families fleeing with what little they could carry; sons still drenched with the sweat of battle, dying in their mothers' arms; orphaned children wandering aimlessly, in shock at the loss of their parents.

These are the kinds of things that those of us who served in Vietnam witnessed and lived through. That we did not write or talk about these horrors was not because we were trying to be strong, silent heroes. We were silent because we cared.

10

WAR AND INTIMACY

THERE ARE GOOD REASONS WHY PEOPLE DON'T OPEN a box of memories. For some it is because the worst of times were, in a strange way, the best of times. For others it is because the memories are too intense, too painful. And for still others it is because we know that those days gone by are part of the past and cannot be explained to those we live with in the present.

For me, it was a case of "all of the above." Only on very rare occasions in the two-and-one-half decades since Vietnam have I delved into my foot-locker full of war memorabilia. I had done so when I wrote my first book, *Under Fire*, and on one or two occasions before but never for more than a few moments. Just long enough to get something I needed, nothing more.

But this time it was different. In trying to discover what Vietnam might have meant to the rest of America, I opened my locker to try to ascertain exactly what Vietnam meant to me. After rummaging around in musty old maps, medals, photos, letters, and notebooks for the better part of an afternoon, three words seem to fit: intensity, people, and places.

The mementoes brought names, places, and events to mind that I hadn't thought of in years. The maps, more than two decades old, were so burned into my memory that I could close my eyes and still put my finger on a particular place. I can't do that today with a map of where I've lived for twenty-five years.

And because the people I remembered had done remarkably brave and courageous things in so many of those places, there was a flood of memories. In the intensity of those days so long ago, relationships had been forged that would never again be replicated in this life. I realized then why so many Vietnam War vets hide this part of their past. Much of what I am today is the consequence of what I was, yet it is so very hard to relate the intensity of that experience to one who did not share it.

How does a man explain to his wife and children that for the better part of a year everything he did, his very survival, was done for, and dependent on, the relationship he had with another group of people that they will probably never meet? And if those words are hard to share with a wife or parent or child, how much more so with contemporary business associates, colleagues, and friends.

That's why those memories are kept locked away

after the intense, year-long experience many of us had in Vietnam, the relationships we established subsequently were pale by comparison. The people we came to know afterward were consciously or unconsciously judged by an unfair standard: how they measured up when compared to those with whom we had served in The War.

At Annapolis and later on at officer's Basic School at Quantico, grizzled veterans constantly reminded us, as fledgling officers: "Don't get too close to your men!" It was said so often that I was fairly convinced that it had to be one of the fundamental axioms of military leadership. And I suppose there is some wisdom in that admonition, for there are times when discipline requires a certain detachment.

But spending a year in a war like Vietnam somehow tempers that postulate of martial remoteness. Such advice might have worked when officers lived in separate billets, ate in separate dining facilities, went home at night to different quarters. But it sure didn't make much sense in Vietnam.

In the war I went to we lived side-by-side, day in and day out. There are 24 hours in a day, 168 hours in a week. Most of us will never spend that much time with those we love most, our families—every minute of every day, for weeks on end. But in Vietnam, month after month, a platoon commander was constantly with his men. He shared their boredom, their hunger, thirst, footsore fatigue, and moments of horror and dread.

The relationships that are built in that kind of environment are those of absolute trust. There is never a moment when others aren't awake, watching, alert to things going on around them. No one can "fake it" in that kind of situation. Life takes on a certain genuine quality that cannot be replicated anywhere else, except perhaps in a lifeboat, lost at sea. You learn very quickly whom you can count on and whom you cannot.

In the many, many hours that men spend together in very difficult circumstances like those in Vietnam, they share some of the deepest, most cherished things they believe in. I heard the Marines of 2d Platoon, men from entirely different backgrounds, places, origins, races, and religions, talk about families, hometowns, plans for the future, disappointments of the past, parents, siblings, friends, lovers, and their faith in and fear of God.

I suspect that many said things to one another that they would never think of sharing with a spouse, or a chaplain, simply because they all faced the same war and its inevitable sad companion—death. Looking back today on those conversations and the intensity of the relationships that they helped forge, it is clear to me that only a fool or a totally insensitive person could fail to get very close to another in such a situation. That's why looking through a footlocker like mine is so difficult.

Just about everybody who spent time in Vietnam, and certainly those of us who were in the infantry out in the field, came to know the gut-twisting sensation of losing one of those with whom we shared so much. It wasn't just that it was someone from the same squad, platoon, or company; the person in that body bag was someone who had carried the same load, walked the same hills, sweated along with us, and who had stayed awake while we slept.

The bonds that are created in war are not the ordinary ones of friendship. They are made of necessity in the struggle to stay alive and get a very difficult job done. You begin to rely on somebody else in a way you never have before and very likely, never will again. In combat, just the simple act of closing your eyes and going to sleep becomes an act of extraordinary trust. For a squad leader or platoon commander, to even be able to go to sleep for perhaps two or three hours is an expression of faith in your fellow man. The same was true of the two-man listening posts that we put outside our perimeters every night on Vietnam's beautiful but godforsaken mountaintops. Those hills were full of people who wanted to kill us. If the guy next to you dozed off while you got some sleep, you could, as the troops would say, "wake up dead." The intimacy and the trust that developed were unavoidable effects of the war and are also a prime reason why it's so painful for people to paw through the memories they have had locked up waiting to be brought into the light once again.

Perusing through that footlocker forced me to look back on a part of my life that I know I'm never going to live through again—nor would I want to—but also left me feeling a little guilty. Guilty because I also know that I would not trade those moments for anything, and a bit ashamed because I know how important those men of 2d Platoon, Kilo Company, were to me, and because it is just something I cannot explain to those with whom I now share my life. From the one or two times since The War that I've been able to talk to other Vietnam veterans about these thoughts, I've concluded that the intensity of that experience touched many who experienced it in a way that is hard to grapple with and virtually impossible to share.

When I was a kid, I remember reading my dad's copies of Bill Mauldin's books about Willie and Joe in WWII. These two cartoon characters were together for everything that war offered. They were close. That's how Jim Lehnert, my radio operator, and I were. For more than six months we were rarely farther apart than the length of a handset cord—about four feet.

Then one day the relationship was severed by virtue of nothing else but the two of us going home—first Jim, then I, to our respective homes and families and careers. We each went back to "the world"—to our own lives and the experiences we had lived before the war brought us together.

Jim went home, went to college, then dental school, and started a family. I went back home to Betsy, a growing family, and advancement in the Marines. Years pass. At Christmas you exchange cards. The celebration of a family event brings a note or a call. On rare occasions you see each other, but you never really touch what that relationship of long ago meant. That's just the way it is: It's there, but it isn't something you talk about.

You don't keep the footlocker for no reason at all. I guess I've moved mine a dozen times. I even re-stenciled it over the years as my rank or unit changed. But I didn't have the inclination to take the time to sit down and go through it.

Others have told me that they couldn't talk about these sorts of things with their wives or children.

"How," one Vietnam vet asked, "can you explain relationships galvanized in terror, the kind of trust and intimacy that war forges, to someone who hasn't been there?" I don't know. I've never shared the contents of my footlocker with my family, either.

HEROES

UNTIL THE INVENTION OF THE BOW AND ARROW, those who died in war usually did so in the midst of furious, close, physical combat. Lives were most often lost by those actively engaged in personally defending themselves, or in directly attacking another. Combat took place within the length of an arm, plus a spear, sword, axe, knife, or lance. Under these circumstances the combatants usually had at least a few moments to prepare for the possibility that the engagement might not end the way they expected.

But in modern warfare, that is often not the case. In fact, relatively few of those who died in combat in Vietnam, or Grenada, or Desert Storm were actually engaged in an act that we would describe as "heroic" at the instant of death. At Con Thien I saw Marines who died when random incoming

89

NVA artillery rounds slammed into a mess tent and killed them as they ate. I saw others who were indiscriminately killed by rockets that ripped them apart as they lay sleeping. Countless others were maimed or killed by anonymous mines or booby traps.

That's not to say that those who died this way—and many others under similar circumstances—were not heroes. In my estimate, they were heroic—by virtue of what they had done days or even moments before, or simply by their very presence in the vicinity of battle, when others had managed to avoid even being in the same country, much less on the battlefield.

And then there were those who died in combat, not in some heroic action but simply doing their jobs under very dangerous circumstances.

On 28 July 1969, Private First Class Frank Coulombe and Captain Mike Wunsch both died this way, within minutes and only yards of each other. Neither the private nor the captain had but a few seconds at most to think about the possibility. Both were doing what they had been trained to do. Neither gave his life. Their lives were taken from them suddenly and with little if any warning of imminent danger. But acts less notable are not necessarily less noble. While neither man was doing anything particularly valiant at the instant his life was suddenly taken, both men had previously demonstrated a hero's greatness. A hero's measure is more than the effect of immediate actions at the moment of death. It is also marked by such qualities as steadfast dedication, commitment, and devotion.

On another level, there were those who knowingly took great risks—of physical injury, or even death—to do something that would save others. Les Shafer was such a hero. On 22 February 1969 our platoon had been assigned to conduct an "RIF"—reconnaissance-in-force—with tanks and armored personnel carriers—"APCs"—northeast of Con Thien. The Marines normally didn't use APCs, but the U.S. Army had somehow loaned four of them to the Corps, and we had trained on them for several days before going out on this little operation to assess the effects of a B-52 raid along the southern border of the DMZ the night before. Late in the afternoon, on our way back to the Con Thien combat base, we inadvertently rolled right into a North Vietnamese Army perimeter, about a kilometer south of the DMZ. Les Shafer died manning a machine gun atop one of the APCs as he covered his squad's deployment from the riddled vehicle. His body was flown back to the United States with the Bronze Star for Valor and a Purple Heart affixed to his casket. Les Shafer was, by the acclaim of his nation, a hero.

So much has been written about heroism that the subject is almost trite—except to those of us who have had the chance to witness it. One of my great blessings in this life is to have been able to be around men like Frank Coulombe, Mike Wunsch, and Les Shafer. And yet, having witnessed real heroism on numerous occasions, I still feel inadequate when I try to describe it to another who was not there.

First, it really isn't accurate to say, as we often do in citations written long afterward, that he "gave" his life for his country. In fact, he didn't "give" it at all. Les Shafer, like all the others I saw die in Vietnam, had his life *taken* from him.

I have no doubt that Les, like me and all those with whom I served, fully intended to survive Vietnam and return home at "end of tour" to friends and family. It is far more accurate to describe the event in which he was killed by saying that he knowingly risked his safety—and his life—to reduce the risk to his men.

In just seconds, with the terrible confusion of sudden enemy fire, the explosions of rocket-propelled grenades, flames, smoke, orders being shouted, and the cries of wounded men, Les Shafer made a decision. The thin-skinned APC holding Shafer and his squad had been disabled by the blast of an RPG. As the largest, most visible stationary target for enemy fire, it was quickly becoming a deathtrap for him and his men, and they needed to get out! He dropped the ramp at the back of the vehicle, ordered his men to exit and spread out around it.

And then Les Shafer made the heroic decision that would cost him his life. He could easily have deployed with his men outside the burning vehicle. But Les was a seasoned squad leader and had been in numerous firefights before this one. His training and experience had taught him that in this kind of a situation troops under fire have a better chance of survival if there is a heavy weapon firing back at the enemy, covering those who are trying to move. The APC gunner, already wounded, could not do what had to be done. No one ordered or asked Les to stay in an exposed position manning the machine gun mounted atop the armored vehicle. But that's exactly what he did. And I watched in horror, through the pain of my own injuries, as he died there, trying the only way he could to diminish the great jeopardy his men were in. Had Les Shafer not covered his men by laying down a heavy base of fire in the midst of that furious fight, our casualties undoubtedly would have been much greater.

I've often wondered what compels a man to willingly do what Les Shafer and so many others like him have done. What makes men take such risks to save a wounded buddy or stand in harm's way or dive on a grenade to save his friends? I don't believe that it is heroism, though Les Shafer was certainly a hero to me.

Few of the Marines, soldiers, sailors, or airmen I have known over a quarter-century of service in the military call it what it is. They call it courage, or esprit, or fancy names like "small unit cohesion." I call it *love*.

Jesus' words in the New Testament put it better than any others I know: "Greater love has no one than this, that he lay down his life for his friends" (John 15:13). That is what Les Shafer did even if he didn't intend to die in the process. He had for his men the kind of love, the kind of intense bond with them, that is forged in steamy jungles and mountainous terrain, during countless forbidding and sleepless nights and the long tedium of shared, sweat-soaked afternoons waiting for a cool night breeze.

Every war is full of stories like these. None of us who have served in combat can ever forget the indelible mark that they leave on us. But those events need not result in the death of the one carrying them out in order for us to be forever changed by bearing witness to them.

Randy Herrod was a hero on that terrible night of July 28, 1969, when he twice raced from the protection of his foxhole to rescue me, shielded my wounded body with his own, and repeatedly remounted his machine gun to beat back an overwhelming attack against our perimeter. What Randy did that night not only very likely saved my life but the lives of many others as well. He could have done less and probably been safer for it.

What made these men do what they did? Courage? Certainly. Love? No doubt. But I know from my own personal experience in similar situations that in the midst of such events those thoughts do not come to the surface to become conscious in the mind. Usually there isn't time to contemplate such things. In other words, heroism probably isn't what the person is thinking about while acting in ways that others describe as heroic.

What motivates people in such ghastly circumstances like those that befell Frank Coulombe, Mike Wunsch, Randy Herrod, or Les Shafer? In addition to love and courage, I think they each possessed another crucial element of human character: faithfulness. In all the "heroic" acts I have been privileged to witness, or even be a part of, there also seemed to be a certain sense of fidelity to people and to purpose. It may well be this particular attribute that brings forth in certain people a recognition, in some cases almost instantly, that *something* has to be done, that doing nothing will not suffice.

In combination, these qualities of courage, love,

and faithfulness are often powerful enough to overcome the innate desire for self-protection or even preservation that we all possess. The end result, amidst conditions that can only be described as horrible, was the kind of heroism that many of us witnessed in Vietnam.

Such qualities are almost unique to those who distinguish themselves in small combat units. A somewhat different but no less courageous motive inspires a fireman to rush into a burning building to save a life, or a policewoman to face down an armed and dangerous criminal, or a pilot to brave the hazards of enemy missiles, guns, and fighters in a solo attack over enemy territory. Yet all of these share a common consequence: The heroic actions of a few nearly always contribute to the accomplishment of a difficult task, the mission at hand.

Even in cases when the heroic act does not succeed, there is usually some good that results. Had Les Shafer's action not saved the lives of his men, the fact that someone might have survived to recount his gallantry would have inspired others to future acts of bravery. Throughout history, stories of heroes—some who succeeded and others who failed—have heartened people and induced them to accomplish greater good. But that didn't happen in Vietnam. Oh, certainly within the small units that did most of the fighting, acts of heroism were awe-inspiring and encouraged others. But they rarely had an effect outside the unit in which they occurred and certainly didn't arouse our nation as a whole to accomplish what we had supposedly set out to achieve.

Therein lies much of the frustration and anger

over Vietnam. Despite the extraordinary courage and sacrifice of so many, in the end the overall mission was not accomplished. That would have been bad enough, but worse still, the valor, so evident in America's courageous sons, resulted in nothing good. There was nothing inspiring, nothing noble, there were no heroes, to motivate and encourage others. In the end it was all for naught.

For twenty-five years that's how I viewed Vietnam. I was convinced that nothing could change the outcome; that those of us who fought there could do little, if anything, to alter the tragic consequences or sense of failure from that dark decade in American history. What I discovered when I finally went back to Vietnam was something entirely different.

My 1993 trip was like a reconnaissance. I saw firsthand how dramatically the situation had changed since I last was there. Our former enemy, the menace of communism, is now more a nuisance than a threat. Yet the tragic consequences of our failure were patently evident in the numerous orphanages filled with homeless and abandoned children, hospital wards overflowing with the sick and maimed, the cities and countryside teeming with people suffering from hardship and economic depression. Limbless former Vietnamese soldiers from both sides of their civil war can be found on street corners the length of the country. Refugee camps in neighboring countries remain filled with those hoping to escape the bitter past and desperate present for a better future. I was painfully reminded that all this was in spite of the extraordinary personal heroism of nearly three million American men and more than 11,000 American women who served nobly to achieve a different outcome.

In 1969 I left Vietnam, convinced that the kind of heroism I had seen on the battlefield had not been matched by a full measure of commitment by our government or even by many of our countrymen. But going back to Vietnam I realized that those of us who lived through The War can best honor the heroes who no longer live, those who are missing, and those still shattered in mind and body from their experience in hell, by faithfulness to our original purpose.

What we need is a recommitment to one of those qualities so essential to heroism in combat: faithfulness. My return to Vietnam persuaded me that we can complete some unfinished business.

We lost the war the first time around. We can't afford to lose it again.

12

OPTING OUT

WE HEARD THE OBSCENE SCREAM OF THE INCOMING salvo of 122mm rockets just before they slammed into Con Thien Firebase. Seconds before, three Kilo Company Marines and I had been walking across the scarred crest of that bald South Vietnamese hilltop. Scrambling for one of the bunkers buried deep beneath the red clay, we may have set a new land speed record. I practically dived down the flight of wooden steps, secretly cursing the engineers for not having built a slide instead. There in the stifling, black heat of the musty bunker, the back of my flak jacket pressed up against the rough 3 x 12-inch timers, the chin strap of my steel helmet gagging me as I gasped for breath, my quiet prayer of thanks with a dozen of my fellow Marines crammed into the shelter, the answer to the insane dilemma of Vietnam became

98

clear: "If we can't go after them when they shoot at us like this, we ought to count our losses and get out while the getting is good."

It was commonplace to view attacks such as these very, very personally. Oh, sure, military shrinks can offer perfectly rational, articulate arguments on why you should never assume that you in particular are the target of a mortar, artillery, or rocket barrage. But when you have just done a footrace to outrun a red-hot blizzard of Soviet-made steel shrapnel fragments, and the final rounds are still plowing into the ground above, it isn't a very convincing presentation. In fact, for those hunkered down in the claustrophobic bowels of a dank bunker, it becomes normal to think in terms like, "those S.O.B.s are trying to kill me, and I can't do a thing about it." There's nothing quite like the fear of God fashioned by incoming enemy artillery round to clear the mind.

At the Naval Academy none of the lecturers ever told us—they certainly didn't tell me—that it was going to be like this. Annapolis and the follow-on Marine Officers Basic Course at Quantico had been all about how to win wars by taking the fight to the enemy. Somehow the instructors had omitted the part about getting used to being pounded on a regular basis by an unseen enemy that you couldn't go after.

I didn't think that I had missed the class that taught us such things. And I sure hadn't forgotten the lessons I'd been taught, for I'd only graduated from Annapolis a little over six months before. And I'd been at Quantico, soaking up tactics, fire support, logistics, and the like, just weeks prior to my windsprint to the bunker. But no one in these institutions of military learning wanted to admit, or even acknowledge, the dirty little secret about the Vietnam War: that we weren't there to win.

That's not to say that I, or any of my fellow 4000 midshipmen at Annapolis, had been in some cloistered environment sheltered from the reality of the world around us. We all avidly read and watched the news coverage coming from Vietnam. We studied operational and after-action reports from the field and felt the slow but steady growth of the antiwar movement outside the gray walls of "the small boat and barge school in Crabtown." None of us could turn on the television or pick up a newspaper or even walk down the streets of Annapolis to Navy/Marine Corps Memorial Stadium without thinking about it. From 1966 onward, The War weighed heavily on the minds of everybody at the Academy. For my last three years, Vietnam was inescapable.

By the mid-1960s, any casual visitor to Annapolis could immediately see, and every midshipman noticed every day, that the military members of the Academy faculty and staff were nearly all veterans of Vietnam. Their telltale personal medals and unit awards preceded them on their uniforms. And, across "the Yard" from the academic area at the Academy, at Bancroft Hall, the dormitory for the all-male Brigade of Midshipmen, nearly all the staff were veterans of Vietnam.

By 1968, large boards trimmed in black had been erected just inside the entrance to Bancroft Hall to serve as a somber memorial to graduates who had been killed in Vietnam. Posted on these boards were rows of postcard-sized photos of graduates who had gone to The War and died in combat—young men who had trod the same corridors only a few years, or in some cases, even months before. Beneath each photo of the deceased graduate was a brief recognition including the write-up that had appeared in his class yearbook and carefully typed below that, the unit he had served with and the conditions under which he had been killed in the line of duty. Week after week, photos were added until there were scores of them and more boards were quietly added to hold the grim evidence of the war's growing toll. These memorials were a sobering, everyday reminder of why we were at the Academy.

It has been my experience that most healthy young men in their late teens and early twenties are fairly well-convinced that they are going to live forever, that they are impervious to damage, downright invulnerable. That's probably why the military has been able to convince considerable numbers of them to face the lethal terrors of combat or to throw their bodies out of perfectly good airplanes, wearing little more than cloth parachutes.

But it is also clear to me that these same young men, at the threshold of fruitful, productive adult lives will, when consistently reminded of the hellish realities of war's carnage, soon begin to have second thoughts about their chosen profession. And that's precisely the effect those memorial boards of photographs had on the Naval Academy's class of 1968.

When I was a midshipman a quarter of a century ago, those of us scheduled to graduate in June had to decide in February on our choice of service and duty assignment. Unfortunately for the class of 1968, "Service Selection Night" that year was right on the heels of the bloody North Vietnamese/Viet Cong Tet Offensive that was raging throughout the length and breadth of South Vietnam.

Suddenly, just before we were to make the decision on which branch of service we wanted, row after row of new photographs appeared on those ominous, black-draped boards in Bancroft Hall. Many of these new photos and write-ups were of men we personally had known. Only days before their photos were affixed to the boards, these young men had been Navy and Marine flyers, infantry, artillery, and armor officers, serving on swift boats, or as SEALs. Most importantly, they had been alive, some newly wed, others with newborn children. Now they were gone. War's irreversible cost in human life was very much on our minds as we walked past those new photos and up the long flight of stairs to Memorial Hall to choose how we would begin our military careers.

I remember sitting down and arguing with a number of classmates who had decided at the last minute to opt for the Navy's Supply Corps. They knew that I had come to the Academy from the Marine Reserves and would be taking my commission in the Corps and many came back at me with comments like, "Hey, Ollie, more power to you, but I don't want to go over there and have my tail shot off." To a man, my classmates were red-blooded American patriots, but the sobering realities of Vietnam displayed on those boards in Bancroft Hall affected the decisions many of them would make that day.

My former roommate was one of those who changed his mind at the last minute. He was a solid, hard-charging, United States Marine Corps sort of guy and we had often talked of serving together. But on Service Selection Night he elected another course. I challenged him, "Look, weren't you the guy who dreamed of being a Marine ever since you got here? You can't fool me. I know you. We've been roommates. We're classmates. We know each other like brothers. Why opt out now?"

I remember his looking me in the eyes and saying, "Hey, get off my back, friend, my fianceé is dead-set opposed to it and I'm going to go in the Navy instead." And so he did. He became a Navy surface-line officer, and a very good one at that. Eventually he was chosen to command the U.S.S. Sequoia, the presidential yacht. And, in ironic twist, he finally left the Navy because of his disappointment with the only graduate of our alma mater to make it to the White House, the man who took one of the most dramatic steps toward trying to reconcile the wounds of Vietnam: President Jimmy Carter.

But in 1968, neither my roommate, nor I, nor most of our class, understood what we would come to realize only later: that we really weren't in the Vietnam war to "win"—at least not in terms that we understood from World War II or even Korea. Nor did any of us, not even gung-ho types, know how terrible it would be to fight in a war that our own government had decided *not* to win.

By the time I was gasping for breath in that hot, dark bunker at Con Thien after only thirty days "in country"—and perhaps my 10th or 15th bout with an enemy we couldn't fight according to "the book"—it was dawning on me that something was terribly wrong. Even a Marine could figure that out. And though no one had told us before we got there, everyone from the lowliest grunt to the general knew it. The trouble was that no one seemed to know what to do about it, or even whom to blame.

As the war ground on and the body counts reported on both sides mounted, blame is what it eventually boiled down to. The politicians blamed the military and especially the media. The antiwar activists blamed the politicians and especially the military. The military blamed the politicians, the media, and especially the antiwar movement.

The troops, of course, concluded that IQ points dropped off quickly the higher one went up the chain of command. But they always reserved a special place in their hearts for certain key figures who had earned the respect from the ranks. Generals like Lew Walt, Ray Davis, and Lew Wilson in the Marines, and the U.S. Army's Dick Stilwell, were heroes and legends in their own right, and held above criticism. So too was "Ol' Westy"—General William C. Westmoreland. Though his vociferous critics quickly forgot, many of the troops remembered that Westmoreland had served "in 'Nam" for four-and-a-half years. He had become the war's single most visible military leader, constantly on TV and in the newspapers. And though he had been ordered home by the time my tour began in late 1968, he was remembered with affection by those who were back for a second tour.

And so if the generals weren't to blame for the

mess we were in, who was? Many said it was all president Lyndon Johnson's fault. And he was an easy target for blame—a convenient scapegoat. I remember watching on television, in the company wardroom at Annapolis, as LBJ announced that he would not seek another term as President. Like so many in our nation, Vietnam had broken him.

By the time I arrived in Vietnam in November 1968, the newly elected president, Richard Nixon, was saying that after his inauguration in January 1969, he would get U.S. forces out of Vietnam. His promise to do just that had helped give him a landslide victory and he clearly meant to keep his word. In the years since, he and I have talked about that pledge and in his book, *No More Vietnams*, he wrote eloquently of the commitments we made to the people of Vietnam and the bitter consequences of breaking them as his administration became embroiled in controversy.

As I sat hunched and helpless in the sweltering confines of a bunker at Con Thien on that day in December 1968, all those events, culminating in the final, catastrophic collapse of the country I was in, were still well in the future. And that was a good thing, because I felt lousy enough as it was.

Sitting there, underground, hiding from the incoming rounds from artillery and rocket launchers that we couldn't cross into North Vietnam to destroy, I didn't feel particularly brave. I knew we weren't going to be allowed to do what we ought to do. And every other soldier, sailor, airman, and Marine in 'Nam knew it, too.

My brother, Jack, a U.S. Army infantry officer a few hundred miles south, in the central highlands, had arrived several months before I had. As his rifle platoon was hammered by enemy units that darted back to their sanctuaries in nearby Laos, he had vented the same frustrations in letters home that we all felt. Perhaps worst of all was the recognition that absolutely no good purpose was being served by the extraordinary sacrifice of so many people.

And the devastation of realizing that our efforts seemed for nought was compounded by another harsh reality. In other wars, the American people on the "home front" actively supported and encouraged the troops overseas and directed their anger at America's enemies. In this war, the American people were visibly venting their anger at those of us who were doing the fighting—characterizing us as the enemy. The antiwar movement was bad enough, but that wasn't the end of it. U.S. politicians made speeches in which they "deplored" our actions, "loathed" our service, and described our conduct as "immoral." Hollywood stars visited North Vietnam and lauded our adversaries from prisons in which American servicemen were held in despicable conditions.

Someone, though we had no idea who, had decided we were not going to go for a victory in The War. And outside of our immediate families and close friends, the American people, in whose name we served, were angry at us for even being there. And, of course, there was absolutely nothing any of us could do about any of this. The unreconciled anger and sense of betrayal that these factors generated in many Vietnam veterans has been one of the most devastating legacies of the Vietnam War.

Sadly, this anger didn't end when we all came home either, though many people recognized the need to make a try at putting it all behind us and moving on. One of the earliest and most visible efforts at reconciliation, and one of the most vivid failures, came at the hand of President Jimmy Carter.

Shortly after he was inaugurated in 1977, President Carter issued a general amnesty, an Executive Order, pardoning all those who had evaded the draft during the Vietnam War. Contrary to his intent, President Carter's action was like a final drop of acid in the deep wounds of Vietnam veterans, the dependents of those still missing, and the survivors of those who had died. The country we had fought in no longer existed. The country we fought for despised us for having done so. And with the stroke of his pen, the new commander-in-chief's amnesty was seen as an endorsement of those who had opted out any way they could while those who did their duty in good conscience had still not been welcomed home by an ungrateful nation.

I'm not sure President Carter ever really understood how bitter many Vietnam veterans and their families were, and still are, over "The Amnesty." Because I was a Naval Academy graduate, as he was, many of my Marine comrades would ask me, as though I had some special insight, why he would do such a thing. "Doesn't he understand," they would say, "how The Amnesty cheapens the sacrifice of so many? What do they teach you guys at Annapolis?"

There is no doubt in my mind that President Carter's motivation sprang forth from his deep religious faith and a belief that his action would help to start a healing process from the many wounds of Vietnam. His moving and articulate statement at the time he issued his Executive Order says as much.

But what he and his advisors misunderstood or underestimated was the depth of feeling that many in America, veterans and civilians alike, had toward those who had fled the country rather than serve. And because of this strong sentiment, The Amnesty never had the effect that President Carter hoped it would.

Nor could it have achieved what Mr. Carter intended, for the deep divisions over Vietnam weren't only the result of fifty or sixty thousand young people's going to Canada or Sweden to avoid serving their country. The anger over Vietnam that cut so deeply into America's conscience and split our society so severely also had much to do with the disastrous outcome of the war, the way it had been prosecuted, and the grossly unfair process by which people were "selected" to participate in it.

If you were in college or graduate school you could get a deferment. If you became a divinity school student you got a deferment. If you were an upper-middle class young man in America there was a very strong likelihood that you could get a deferment. And yet poorer Americans universally served when drafted because they didn't have the right social or economic status to be deferred.

As a result, our armed forces were chock-full of people who would have taken a deferment if they could have gotten one, but they simply couldn't. They just didn't have the political clout or economic leverage. So, to the extent that it was to be fought, they fought the war for all of us.

And while many of the young men drafted into this brutal experience did not have the education or background of their more privileged countrymen, by the time they returned they were wise enough to know that they had been unwilling participants in a national calamity. What they could not comprehend is why they should be blamed for its conduct or its consequences. And while they were still grappling with the memories of dead and wounded comrades in arms, The Amnesty, rather than healing, hurt them further and deepened their sense of isolation.

They were depicted as pot-headed marauders, when in fact they knew that they were generally decent, courageous young men who had been given little choice but to go when their numbers came up in the draft lottery. In books, articles, TV "documentaries" and films, their heroic sacrifices were portrayed as mindless brutality. Their leaders in combat were caricatured as cruel, incompetent, ruthless martinets. From 1966 on, all of them had returned from The War as they had gone, one at a time. There were no welcome-home parades and until The Wall was dedicated in 1982, there was no national recognition whatsoever.

In the end, most simply tried to step back into "The World" they had left and resume the cadence of everyday life, to put The War and its memories into footlockers with cherished letters, old uniforms, and fading photos. Few, if any, felt reconciled to what had happened. Others, hurt, bitter, disillusioned, and angry, felt that they no longer fit in a society that knew little of what they had endured and simply wanted to forget the whole "Vietnam experience." One at a time, these sad off-spring of the only war America ever lost, did what so many of their contemporaries had done when The War was on—they opted out.

13

A DIVIDED GENERATION

WHEN I LEFT THE STATES IN THE LATE FALL OF 1968, the social and political climate was getting really nasty. During the spring and summer of 1968 many of America's cities weathered some of the worst riots in the nation's history, certainly since our Civil War. The turbulent crosscurrents of racial unrest and dissension over our involvement in Vietnam had erupted into a national crisis. Supposedly there were good reasons for all the burning, bashing, and killing: the murder of Martin Luther King, Jr., power shortages during oppressive heat waves, the Democratic and Republican Parties' National Conventions, and of course, The War. By the time I got on a chartered 707 for my mind-numbing flight across the Pacific for Vietnam, it seemed like the phrase, "Hell, NO! I won't GO!"

was a steady chant that echoed and resounded from a thousand campuses and streets across America.

While in Vietnam, we were at least spared the nightly dose of peace protests, draft card- and flag burnings, and sit-ins that were being beamed into America's living rooms on TV. Though we could read about these events in the occasional *Stars and Stripes* articles, when the newspaper made it to the field, these conditions back home seemed remote and far away.

But the best source of news was the letters we got from home. The mail from "the world" almost always contained clippings from local newspapers. And while a soldier, sailor, airman, or Marine would likely keep the handwritten pages from loved ones to himself, the clippings would usually get circulated throughout the squad or platoon. It was not at all unusual, on a long, boring afternoon, to find yourself poring over a thumb-worn news clipping about a Little League team in a town you had never heard of, or the details of a wedding between two people you would never meet in a place you would never visit.

In a strange sort of way, these clippings, received sporadically from all over America, gave us a better feel for what was really going on across the length and breadth of our land than if we had been at home reading a major metropolitan newspaper. And, of course, interspersed among the local lore, the obituaries, the local weather, there, too, would be the stories about the riots, the protests, the burnings, the national uproar over The War.

Nobody seemed to call it the "Vietnam Conflict," anymore. It was just The War. The Hateful, Napalm

Flaming, Baby Killing, Hooch Burning, Civilian Destroying, No Good, Lousy, Stinking War!

That's why coming home from the war wasn't exactly everything it was cracked up to be. Oh, don't get me wrong, I was glad to be coming home. Glad to be coming back to my lovely wife and our baby girl I'd not yet held. Glad to be alive, in one piece. Glad to see my parents, her parents, my brothers and sister, her sisters. Glad to see just about anybody who didn't want to kill me.

I knew it was going to be nice not to awaken, heart racing in the pre-dawn hours of the night, not to have to dig a hole before lying down, not to have to eat out of a green can, drink 100-degree water out of a canteen full of iodine, not to smell like a goat, not to kick the person next to you for snoring loud enough to get you killed.

I looked forward to the sweet scent and softness of the woman I loved, to showers, to sleeping in a real bed with clean sheets, to living in a house with real doors, to cold milk, fresh vegetables, bread, cold beer, clothes that didn't stink, shoes that didn't weigh ten pounds from walking in mud and water day and night, and going places without wondering if the person coming toward you is going to try to kill you.

Oh, during your tour there were so many things to look forward to and dream about when coming home. But then you remembered that no one you were going to meet understood what you had missed, what you had experienced. What it was like to cradle the bleeding body of a dying Marine in your arms. And you knew, even before you tried, that you couldn't possibly explain it—the smells, the fears, the impressions, the uncertainties. That if you tried, it would somehow take away their joy, their happiness at your being home. And so, you didn't even try.

Instead, every once in a while, even in your bliss at being home, you would sometimes feel like crawling out of your skin, as though you didn't deserve to be in it, remembering that there were others whom you had known and known well, who wanted what you now had as much as you, and that they would never have it. And sometimes, just for no reason at all, you would go into a room just to be alone, to remember, and to cry. Every once in a while, when I first came home, early in the morning when I got up to shave, having lathered my face and begun to draw the blade over my beard, I would find myself crying, the tears running down my face, making streaks in the shaving soap.

Why? I would silently ask myself. "I have it made. I have a wonderful wife, a beautiful daughter, another child on the way." I was doing what I loved: leading and teaching young Marines. "What's wrong with you, North?"

When I came back from Vietnam at the end of 1969, there hadn't been any brass bands playing or welcome-home banners. Fortunately, there were no protestors awaiting me either when I stepped off the plane in Pittsburgh to hugs and kisses from Betsy, her family, and our little baby.

After a month's leave time, we moved into quarters "aboard" the sprawling Marine Corps Base at Quantico, Virginia, about fifty miles south of Washington. Our neighbors were just like us: young married Marines with families and small children. Many of us in the neighborhood were instructors, just back from Vietnam. Our job was to teach and train other Marines who were headed for the war from which we had just returned.

But even in this protected, insulated environment there were signs of serious trouble. When I had left for Vietnam in 1968, everyone in the military openly traveled in uniform. Now, we were told not to leave base in anything but civilian attire, as if our uniforms and ribbons were a public mark of disgrace. The new Marine lieutenants we were teaching had it even tougher than we "old salts." Orders came down to avoid the "areas of confrontation." For the student lieutenants, that meant Washington D.C. Most of them were bachelors, and trying to get a date with a short haircut in those days had to be next to impossible.

In "bull sessions" my fellow instructors and I would often congratulate ourselves for being married because the average Marine, soldier, sailor, or airman was having anything but fun on liberty. Those of us who had "been there" had our wives and each other. But the new officers and troops, just a few years younger, and preparing to go to The War, were effectively isolated from the mainstream of society. By 1970, the antiwar movement had succeeded in dividing a generation.

Most of us were the sons and daughters of parents who had weathered the Great Depression and then endured World War II. The Russians called the Second World War "The Great Patriotic War." It was also that here—every family was affected in one way or another, either in combat, by the rationing, or at the very least, by the war effort. Our parents had also been motivated and encouraged by the very effective media campaign organized by the Roosevelt and Truman administrations. The American people were galvanized behind those who went to fight the Axis. And, though lower in volume and more temperate in rhetoric, a similar effort had been organized five years after World War II, when the U.S. became involved in Korea.

Because the American people perceived that the Korean War had begun with the same kind of unprovoked aggression that they had witnessed at Pearl Harbor, there was significant support when President Truman dispatched the first troops to the Asian peninsula to check the advances of the North Korean Communists. In short order, many of those who had served in World War II were called back into service for duty in Korea. And even after the Chinese entered the war and the conflict bogged down in a lethal stalemate along the 38th parallel, no serious antiwar effort was ever mustered.

Vietnam was different. The war didn't start with naked aggression as did World War II or Korea. The American people didn't understand this insurgency in the jungle. They were never convinced that the people of Vietnam were worth American blood, or that the Communist seizure of all of Southeast Asia ever posed a serious threat to this nation. Thus, Vietnam became an easy war to hate. And the warriors who fought in it became easy targets for impassioned anger and armchair criticism.

Perhaps the only other event in our nation's history that stirred such passion and protest was our own very "Un-Civil War Between the States."

When Abraham Lincoln was elected in 1860, there were some major protests, but after the South seceded, even these disorders paled by comparison to the civil disturbances that occurred in New York and Chicago when he suspended *habeas corpus*. The draft riots of the 1860s were deadly, damaging, and visceral, just like the angry response that Vietnam evoked 110 years later.

By the time I was teaching new lieutenants at Quantico, American involvement in the Vietnam War had been dragging on for the better part of eight years—longer than our own bloody War of Independence. It had become a genuine quagmire of monumental proportions. And while it is never wise to ascribe "national characteristics" to a people, it is safe to say that Americans are generally an impatient lot. By 1970 "We, the People" were simply fed up. It had gone on too long. It was going nowhere. There was no resolution in sight, no proverbial light at the end of the tunnel. The endless, weekly "body-counts" and the probing eye of the television, blasting the war into America's living rooms, had taken too great a toll on the corporate consciousness of America.

Many Americans, especially the young, vented their frustration and anger against the most visible manifestation of war—those of us in uniform. We were easy targets. In so doing, they were directly confronting their peers—just as in our Civil War. And like our own war that pitted north against south, the civil war in Vietnam was being fought in every conceivable venue: on battlefields, on college campuses, in living rooms, in the halls of Congress, and on our city streets. And like our Civil War, the

Vietnam War divided Americans and pitted them against each other.

Sadly, the analogy ends there. When our Civil War ended, a reunified America set out to heal its wounds and restore a divided generation. But the kind of reconciliation that Abraham Lincoln so fervently sought to achieve evaded us in the wake of Vietnam. As if to perpetuate the tragedy that began in the emerald valleys and steamy rice paddies and tangled jungles of Vietnam, the wounds The War created in America continued as a festering abscess in our country long after we withdrew from Southeast Asia.

When it ended, each man or woman touched by the poisonous anger of The War went his or her own way and the country ambled on under the effects of the so-called Vietnam Syndrome, neither truly healed nor fully reconciled. The fighting may be over in the jungles a half a world away, and protest marches might have stopped in the streets at home, but the dark shadows that The War cast and the burning coals of the anger it ignited have endured too long. These lingering vestiges of Vietnam—now a full generation removed, still remain—and efforts to erase or ignore them have not worked.

In 1991, President George Bush, after the decisive victory by U.S.-led forces in Desert Storm declared that the Vietnam Syndrome was finally behind us. For those soldiers, sailors, airmen, and Marines who had served in both Vietnam and Desert Storm, he was very likely right. These professional warriors had proven that given the chance, they could do what they had been trained and equipped to do—and what they hadn't been allowed to do in Vietnam. Desert Storm also made it clear that the lessons of Vietnam had indeed been learned in Washington. Gone were the days of micromanagement from the corridors of power. Gone were arcane "limited engagement" rules, "free-fire" zones and "Don't shoot unless shot at" policies. In Desert Storm the military planners were allowed to fight the enemy without one hand tied behind their backs as they had been in Vietnam.

But when the victors of Desert Storm returned to ticker-tape parades and the welcoming embrace of a grateful nation, one could also hear the angry mutterings among Vietnam vets about "unlimited air power," "hundred hour warriors," the enemy army being "the mother of all cowards," and "where was *my* parade?" Sour grapes, say some. Yet, these are still signs that many of those who fought in Vietnam do not feel at all vindicated by the extraordinarily swift victory of the Persian Gulf war.

There is a difference between learning the hard lessons of that earlier experience and putting its anger, sadness, and tragic consequences behind us. Desert Storm did indeed prove that we had done the former. It also showed that we had not yet achieved the latter. The dilemmas created by our involvement in Vietnam are still far from resolved or reconciled.

Some believed that the 1992 election of a president, who as a young man had evaded the draft and protested against The War, would be a catalyst for the healing so much sought for by so many. But even that has failed to work. Instead, much like President Carter's amnesty, the election of Bill

Clinton has reopened old wounds from Vietnam, further polarized thinking about The War, and stoked the anger of many.

The hostile greeting Mr. Clinton received at The Wall on Memorial Day 1993 is ample evidence of the deep persistence of The War's unreconciled anger.

The fact is, no single act by any president or political leader is likely to close the deep wounds of Vietnam or salve its ugly scars. The kind of serious healing that is so much needed can only come from a consistent pattern of behavior by many. And those who are best suited to start this process of reconciliation are those of us who served there and endured the long night of "Nam."

14

STILL WOUNDED

Washington, D.C.: 1984

"WELCOME HOME," THE BEARDED MAN IN THE camouflage jacket said as I jogged past him on the Mall. It was November 1984, just a few days after President Reagan's Veteran's Day dedication of Frederick Hart's "Three Fightingmen" statue at the Vietnam Veterans Memorial, and this slightly built, long-haired, and apparently homeless man was standing alone on the sidewalk, stoop-shouldered, seemingly with no place to go. I waved and kept jogging but then noticed a group of four others, similarly attired, equally unkempt, just standing in the cold beside the pool, east of "The Wall," hands in pockets with no apparent purpose except to be there.

There was no pretense of hostility or malevolence, nothing sinister about these men. But I was overcome by a sudden sense of sadness and it killed the enthusiasm I had for running back to the Secret Service gym in the basement of the Old Executive Office Building, next door to the White House.

I stopped running and turned to the man who had greeted me, my breath turning to mist in the late autumn chill. The man hadn't moved, hadn't even turned when I passed. He was still just standing there, looking toward The Wall. As I walked back to him, I noticed that from where he stood, you couldn't even see The Wall—just the cut that it made in the leaf-covered green of the lawn.

When I got back to the man, I noticed that the jacket he wore had several unit patches neatly sewn on the back, shoulders, and breast pockets. Some designated various U.S. Army commands, one was the black and silver POW/MIA patch, and yet another proclaimed the wearer to be a Disabled Vietnam Veteran. "Why did you say that?" I asked.

"You were there, weren't you?" he replied.

"Yes, I was. But how did you know?"

"Because you look like you were there," was his answer.

By now, the other four who had been standing quietly by the pool had walked over to us. One of them said, almost in a whisper—"He's not messin' with you is he?"

I didn't know which one of us was being addressed and turned toward them, but as I did, the veteran I had been talking to said, "No, he's not messin' with me. We were just talkin' about it. This guy was an officer."

Taken aback, I asked, "How do you know that?"

"You were, weren't you?"

"Yes, but again, how did you know that?" I was wearing a pair of running shorts, a gray sweatshirt, and running shoes. No name. No sign of rank. I was fascinated.

"No matter, I just know, that's all. Like I said, 'Welcome Home.'"

"Welcome home to you, too. Tell me, what are you doing here?" By now, I'd recovered my breath and was more than a little curious about these five men, all bearded, long haired, thin to the point of being scrawny, and all dressed generally the same. Each man wore a Vietnam-era camouflage jacket, all had a variety of unit patches and the POW/MIA patch. Three wore military jungle boots, the kind we wore in Vietnam. One had a U.S. Marine Corps insignia—the eagle, globe, and anchor—on a pocket flap and a tattered USMC field cap, what we called a "utility cover," over his long hair. All wore threadbare jeans that were, at best, several weeks away from a laundry. All appeared to be in their mid-thirties, I guessed.

"We're just watchin'," said the one who had asked if I had been "messin'" with his colleague. He quickly established himself as the new spokesman for the group.

"Watching what?" I asked.

"Just watchin', you know. Just watchin' to see who was comin' by to see our buddies. Were you an officer over there like John says you were?"

"Yes, I was, but how does he know and why does that matter?" I inquired.

"It's good for you officers to come here and see what you done, that's all."

His words were said without malice or rancor, but they hit me like a punch, and I could feel myself coloring. "Why do you say that?" I asked.

"Because you officers were the ones who did it. You're the ones who left 'em there. You're the ones who wasted 'em."

There it was again: *wasted*. The one word that was sure to bring a rush of memories back to anyone who had served in that particular hell. That one word summed up more than 58,000 lives, the expending of a national treasure, and more than a decade of blood and grief.

I stayed for a few more minutes, trying to engage these five men in conversation. Where were they from? Where and when did they serve? What did they do now?

The one with the Marine cover said he had served with the 3d Marine Division. Another said he had been a Navy corpsman—a field medic—with a swift boat detachment in "the Delta"—the Mekong River Delta. Two claimed to have been with the 82d Airborne and were wearing parachutists "jump wings"—the airborne insignia—as if to prove it. The fifth, bearing a Bronze Star, a Purple Heart, and an Army Air Medal on his chest, said he had served with a helicopter unit in the "Air Cav"—an air cavalry regiment.

They all spoke quietly, using the acronyms familiar only to those who had been there, or at least those who followed the war closely. None of them was from Washington, yet all had been there for months. In near mumbles, they each admitted that none of them had homes, jobs, families, or any of the other connections most of us take for granted.

One by one they had found each other here at The Wall. They occasionally visited a homeless shelter for food and protection from the elements, always together.

After a few minutes, we exhausted any common ground and we parted. As I left, two or three said "welcome home," again; as if this was both a greeting and a good-bye.

I jogged back toward the White House grounds for a few hundred yards, and once across Constitution Avenue and out of sight I stopped and walked. The fun had gone out of my noontime run.

Though they said "welcome home," these men really weren't home. They were still stuck in Vietnam. None of them had any purpose in life except to be with their buddies—those on The Wall and these other living, like-minded casualties of that long-ago war. All of these men had been in Vietnam at roughly the same time that I had served there. And what they had said troubled me.

These five men had clearly been unable to put their experiences behind them—and now they had dragged out some of my memories from the footlocker in which I had so carefully stored them. In the days after this meeting on the Mall, I began to resent their intrusion into my memories. I had carefully tucked Vietnam away in the dark recesses of my mind, a half-decade before. It was part of me, but over, done, finished. Or so I thought.

The men I'd met by The Wall that day had dragged my footlocker out and made me think about the names I knew but had only glanced at, etched into the black granite. I'd stopped once, to say a brief prayer of remembrance—but nothing more. The five men I met that day in 1984 apparently spent hours each day re-living their Vietnam experiences—and dwelling on comrades who had been "wasted."

In the weeks that followed, that word—*wasted*—would come back to haunt me in a melancholy way.

At work, President Reagan was engaged in another effort to convince the Congress to restore funds for the armed resistance in Nicaragua—the Contras.

Vietnam would be mentioned—in papers prepared by the NSC staff, where I served; in comments by the president; and, by Contra supporters and opponents in both the Administration and the Congress.

Those who advocated support for the guerrilla army that the U.S. had helped create in Nicaragua would say things like: "We can't abandon these people like we did the Vietnamese."

Opponents of aiding the Contras and much of the media took the opposite Vietnam tack: We're on the slippery slope toward U.S. military involvement, in another jungle war, just like Vietnam."

For those of us in the government who had served in Vietnam, whether we were now in Congress, at the Pentagon, the State Department, the CIA, or even on the White House or NSC staff—these reflections back to this long ago, faraway war had special meanings. Undoubtedly, each of us were affected differently, but for me, I was repeatedly reminded of that haunting word: *wasted*.

And it wasn't only the government. The civil war in Nicaragua and spreading Communist insurgencies in Central America were viewed by many private citizens and nongovernment organizations with the same kinds of passions that Vietnam had stirred.

As in the government, activists on both sides of the issue became intensely engaged in promoting their particular perspective. Peace activists, student organizations, and quasi-political groups deployed legions of supporters to the region in support of the Sandinistas in Nicaragua and the FMLN guerrillas in neighboring El Salvador.

Many of those engaged on both sides of this heated debate were veterans of the Vietnamese experience. They had been adversaries over the conduct of the Vietnam War—and now they were opponents again over America's role in Central America. But even in their heated, often acrimonious dispute over what if any role the United States should be playing in El Salvador, Honduras, Guatemala, or Nicaragua, there was one thing that both sides could agree on: Nobody wanted another Vietnam.

Does the common thread of Vietnam tie together the actions of those of us involved in the covert effort to help the Nicaraguan Resistance after their funding was cut off by Congress? I can't answer for Bud McFarlane, Admirals Poindexter or Moreau, or Generals Gorman, Secord, or Singlaub. Nor do I know exactly what motivated brave men in our Central American embassies or their former colleagues from the CIA or even civilians like Rob Owen. But I do know that Vietnam had been a factor in all their lives. And in mine, too.

Notwithstanding all that people later wrote and said about me, my motivation for wanting to help the Nicaraguan Resistance prevail was much simpler and far more selfish than many realized: I did not want my son to have to go fight in another protracted war that was likely to have the same kind of thankless ending as the one in which I had fought.

Everytime we reviewed the classified contingency requirements for U.S. Marines and soldiers to fight a Communist insurgency in Central America, I recalled the words of one of those five men I'd met by The Wall on my noontime run: "You officers were the ones who did it. You're the ones who left 'em there. You're the ones who wasted 'em."

To me the issue was fairly straightforward. President Reagan had found a way to support the Contras that didn't require American troops to fight beside them. If the Nicaraguan Resistance failed, there was no doubt that there could easily be a war involving U.S. troops in Central America. By all estimates, such a war would be a long one. And my son, Stuart, would soon be registering for the draft. Even the most optimistic projections of such a war anticipated a protracted, bloody affair that might well end in the same way as Vietnam, and I didn't want that to happen. In other words, I did not want my son, or any other Americans, for that matter, to be "wasted" in the jungles of Nicaragua.

Later, long after the Nicaraguan War was over and I was working on this book, I was again reminded of those five men whom I had met by The Wall. My son—and perhaps thousands of others—had indeed been spared being *wasted*.

Did any of those five men I had met on that noontime run in 1984 realize that they, too, were "wasted"? What had happened to them? Was it because one day they were teenaged kids throwing baseballs in a sandlot, and a few months later they were throwing grenades in rice paddies or on jungle-covered mountains? Was it because they just couldn't cope with the hostility that greeted them when they returned?

I've thought a lot about that meeting since that day on the Mall. Several times afterward, on my noontime runs, I looked for them. And though I couldn't find the same five again, I've certainly found many others like them, dressed in similar garb. Almost all these men have one item in common—the POW/MIA patch. Now, whenever I'm at some kind of patriotic event, say a 4th of July celebration, I look for other battered veterans like those five. They're hard to miss. You can see them at almost any public gathering in a major metropolitan area—though they seem to be rarer in rural settings.

Who are they? Why do they seem so lost? Where were their counterparts after World War I, World War II, or Korea?

These "walking wasted" veterans of this long ago, far away war may even be but a small though highly visible part of a much larger picture. The available statistics paint a gruesome legacy:

— Today, the Vietnam War Memorial has 58,191 names engraved on it. In the late 1980s, a study published in the *New England Journal of Medicine* estimated that as many Vietnam war veterans may have committed suicide as died in Southeast Asia.

— Though no government study of federal, state, and local confinement facilities is available, Chuck

Colson's Prison Fellowship estimates that between 100,000 and 200,000 Vietnam veterans are incarcerated in America's prisons and at least that many are on parole. A 1981 study showed that one in four Vietnam vets had been arrested for a criminal offense. There are 147 known Vietnam vets, and possibly as many as 200, on death row.

— According to the 1988 *National Vietnam Veterans Readjustment Study*, a congressionally mandated report released by the Research Triangle Institute, 14 percent of those who served in Vietnam (one in seven) *still* have serious, psychological problems—Post Traumatic Stress Disorder (PTSD)—directly related to the Vietnam War, and of these veterans, nearly 70 percent have been divorced at least once.

If these numbers are as accurate as their authors believe, why and how could that be?

I'm sure that the great experts on these matters have developed some profound theories on why so many Vietnam veterans are so troubled so long after the war's end. Hopefully, honest veterans will continue to contribute to these analyses so that there will be two very practical consequences: some real help for those who need it, and, steps taken to ameliorate these effects for the veterans of future wars.

In that spirit, let me suggest some possibilities, none of them particularly pleasant, for why so many of those who fought in Vietnam are among the "walking wasted."

First, Vietnam is the first war we've ever really lost. We won all the battles but still lost the war. No matter what anyone says about being a "good loser," nobody likes losers, especially in America. Here, we idolize winners and scorn losers. Oh sure, some will say Korea was a stalemate, or that Desert Storm wasn't a clear-cut victory. Perhaps, but we sure didn't lose them. Nobody can argue that we didn't lose in Vietnam.

Second, the only veterans who returned from Vietnam to a "heroes' welcome" were the POWs. The POWs came back as a group in 1973 to a month-long celebration with flags, cameras, and waiting friends and families. Everyone else who did their year in hell came back as individuals to be spat on, pilloried in the press, condemned on college campuses, and relegated to near criminal status unless they joined a protest organization like the Vietnam Veterans Against The War. In order to find "acceptance" (outside an immediate family or small, rural community) it almost seemed necessary to burn a flag along with the ribbons and medals given for having served there. As if to prove the point, some who did just that were promptly elected to public office.

Third, there were many men who, because of Vietnam's rapid medical evacuation and the remarkable advances in trauma treatment, survived terrible wounds and injuries. In other wars, many of those so severely wounded would have died, but in Vietnam they lived. The survival of these combat casualties left a host of men with major, long term, medical and health problems, trying to cope in a society generally unappreciative of the sacrifices they had made. In other wars, wounded veterans returned to their communities and were accorded honor for their service. Those who lost limbs and eyes and hearing—or worse—in Vietnam had their losses compounded by being cast as suckers for having gone. In 1975, with the collapse of the Republic of Vietnam, these terribly injured veterans were confronted with the reality that they had been wounded in vain. And by 1976, with President Carter's amnesty for those who had evaded service during The War, the disfigured and disabled were forced to survive with the knowledge that they need not have gone at all let alone paid such a terrible price.

Fourth, the typical "grunt" in Vietnam was subject to a much more protracted period of intense risk than his counterpart in most other wars. That's not to say that the actual fighting was heavier or worse than World War I, World War II, or Korea, but the non-stop duration was greater in Vietnam. With some notable exceptions (WWII's Bataan, Corregidor, Guadalcanal, "the Bulge," and the Pusan perimeter and Chosin Reservoir in Korea) most of modern warfare has involved units that were carefully prepared, cast into fierce but relatively brief days or weeks of battle, and then withdrawn to relatively safer areas for rest, refit, and replacement. In Vietnam, most junior officers spent six or seven months "in the field" before being rotated to a higher echelon or a staff assignment. But a typical infantryman, field radio operator, field corpsman or medic, mortarman, rocket man, or machine gunner in Vietnam could expect 350 to 380 days in hell.

And there is another, perhaps more troubling, explanation of why so many who came back from the Vietnam War have had such a hard time adjusting after their experience: Many Vietnam Vets really are "different" from their counterparts who served in and survived America's other modern conflicts.

The Vietnam War was waged in the midst of an era of extraordinary social engineering that began with Lyndon Johnson's "Great Society" initiatives. The consequence of some of these idealistic experiments was to produce a force of younger soldiers, sailors, airmen, and Marines who were less representative of our overall society than in other wars. Most of the young infantrymen who served in rifle platoons like mine in the Marines or my brother's in the U.S. Army, were the sons of America's working poor who could not qualify for a college deferment. They were enticed into the Armed Forces by the promise of a better future, educational benefits, or a letter from their draft boards. On average they were nineteen to twenty years of age, making them five to six years younger than those who served with my father in WWII.

The age and societal background factors alone would have made the fighting force in Vietnam dramatically different from that of other wars, but there was one other factor that, by the time I arrived in 1968, had radically altered the make-up of America's military—the requirement from Washington that the Armed Forces accept significant numbers of men into the ranks who, in any other war, could never have gotten in.

When the "cohort" of eligible, qualified young men began to dry up in the mid- to late-'60s, the civilian leadership of the Pentagon, over the objections of the Joint Chiefs of Staff, simply changed the rules. Young men who previously would have been rejected at local induction centers for mental, medical, physical, or even moral reasons were now deemed to be acceptable. The so-called Project 100,000, developed by Defense Secretary McNamara, brought into the force well over that number of "Category IV," inductees who had heretofore been unable to achieve minimum scores on standardized mental tests. Because in many cases these recruits could not qualify for jobs requiring technical skills, they ended up as infantrymen.

For those who survived the horror of The War, all of these factors combined to make the returning Vietnam Vet generally less "acceptable" in American society than his counterpart in other wars. And even today, more than two decades after the last combat units departed Vietnam, many of these vets still have not experienced the profound meaning of the words "Welcome Home."

15

WHEN SAIGON FELL, WE ALL FELL

COMING HOME FROM VIETNAM AT THE END OF 1969 didn't mean that you were through with the war—or that it was through with you.

For those who "got out"—left the service and returned to civilian life—there was no leaving the war behind. Every night on the family TV and every morning on the front page of the daily paper—news of Vietnam was there.

For those of us who stayed in, the war was an every-day part of training, practice, writing, and planning.

At the giant Marine base in Quantico, Virginia, every instructor was a recent "returnee" eager to pass on his tips on leadership, tactics, and survival to the young officers who would be graduating in months. And even though the 3d Marine Division was now out of Vietnam, the 1st Marine Division was still there, and so were hundreds of advisors. Thus, for the next three years, 1970 – 73, I spent most of every day teaching tactics to, and many nights on field exercises with, young lieutenants —any or all of whom could soon find themselves facing exactly what I had been through.

For Betsy, there was no such involvement. For her, it was a time of making a home for our daughter, and soon after, our son. They helped her mask the anxiety of knowing that if the war continued, her husband and the father of her children would eventually be sent back to that dark well of uncertainty. Her total focus was on our children and our home.

At the end of 1973 my orders came, not back to the war as an advisor but once again to the 3d Marine Division, now on the island of Okinawa.

I spent the year of 1974 on Okinawa, most of it as the officer-in-charge of a small, specialized training unit on the northern tip of the island. It was a terrific experience. It was also the precursor to a near disaster, but I didn't know it at the time. To be the officer-in-charge of the island's Northern Training Area (NTA) was the kind of challenge and responsibility I craved.

It offered me the chance to do all of the exciting things that the Marine Corps uses in its recruiting commercials. We conducted mountain warfare training, ran jungle warfare tactics, taught night amphibious raids in rubber boats launched from navy ships and submarines, rappelled from helicopters, parachute-jumped with U.S. Army and Marine reconnaissance units, taught our pilots and air crews survival skills, and ate snakes and devoured other jungle edibles just to impress the recent arrivals to the Western Pacific. We had a glorious time.

In ten months every combat unit in the region that might be recommitted to combat in Vietnam or sent to fulfill any of a dozen other contingency plans went through the training program run by this little detachment. General Lew Wilson, then the Commanding General of all the Marines in the Pacific theater, was so impressed with what was being accomplished that he gave our little detachment a unit commendation. He also invited the Secretary of the Navy, Bill Middendorf, to inspect the program. When the Secretary arrived, we took him to a training site and he went rappelling down the side of a mountain.

The NTA was a tiny, practically autonomous unit stuck at the far northern end of Okinawa Island—more than thirty miles by dirt roads from any other base. There were no telephones, only radio communications, and they only worked part of the time until one of my gunnery sergeants "appropriated" an old Army communications van and jury-rigged it to work with true Rube Goldberg ingenuity. Everything about the place was sporadic—the electric power, the deliveries of supplies and mail, and the availability of time off. Since training went on twenty-four hours a day, seven days a week, the only time the men could take a break was when we didn't have a unit aboard. And during these periods, most of our days were consumed with repairing our equipment—the rubber boats, climbing lines, and safety gear—and catching the poisonous Habu snakes we used in teaching survival skills.

There was another important factor in this assignment for me. I had previously trained every one of the lieutenants on the island at The Basic School. It was therefore much easier for me to relate to these young officers than it was for many other captains. I knew these lieutenants from Quantico, and most remembered me warmly. As the various units in the Division rotated through the NTA, I was able to handpick the officers who wanted to join me as instructors and staff. Vince Norako, Pete Van Hooser, Bo Wagner, Bob Anderson, and Gil Macklin were among them. We would stay in touch for years afterward.

About two-thirds of the way through my tour, things were running so smoothly that I had the opportunity to take some leave. Instead of going back to the States, I encouraged Betsy to come to Okinawa so that we could take some leave on the island and then go to Tokyo for a few days.

She did. But a major Pacific typhoon arrived just after she did, so our planned trip to Tokyo had to be postponed and cut short while I returned to the NTA to supervise damage repair from the storm and get the training schedule back on track. She came with me.

Betsy's trip to Okinawa was a bittersweet experience. It was wonderful to be with her again after so many months. We talked, played, swam, hiked, sailed, slept, and she even rappelled. But I was also deeply bothered by the rapidly deteriorating situation in Southeast Asia. Clearly, the South Vietnamese government was under enormous pressure. It was becoming apparent that unless the U.S. intervened—as various agreements provided—the

Republic of Vietnam would cease to be. All Marine combat units had been out of Vietnam since 1971. But we still had advisors with the South Vietnamese, and the intelligence reports were not good. Colonel Bill Fitzgerald, the 3d Division operations and training officer, and the man I worked most directly for, invited me to attend several contingency planning conferences at the Division Headquarters, and I flew down by helicopter for these meetings.

The principal reason for my attending these planning sessions was to tailor our training to the division's mission requirements. And we did. Back at the NTA we reoriented our training to focus more on evacuation operations, survival skills, escape and evasion, and the like. We were getting ready in case the division had to go back to Vietnam.

By the late summer of 1974 we all knew that the economic and military aid the U.S. had promised the South Vietnamese government when we pulled out was not going to be forthcoming. We also realized by then that without U.S. intervention—or at least the very real threat of it—the cause so many of us had fought for was lost. By the fall of 1974 it was only a matter of time.

Those of us who had fought there, who still had friends there—both American advisors and Vietnamese we had come to know and admire—didn't understand. We all thought we should be going back. But we were too far from home and too detached from the corridors of power in Washington to understand what had happened in our nation's capital. The Congress, seizing on the Nixon administration's weakness—the deepening

Watergate quagmire—threw up a thousand reasons why it would no longer fund the war—regardless of the promises the administration had made during the "peace talks."

Half a world away we thought we knew better. Even though the Congress had cut U.S. military and economic aid to the South Vietnamese to a trickle, the president still had the authority to send in the Marines—and surely he would do so before all those lives and all the sacrifice of ten years of war were wasted.

From my vantage point at the division planning meetings it was apparent that the end was nearing in Vietnam. The U.S. Army had even reopened Camp Hardy, their Special Forces base, south of my base camp on Okinawa's east coast. It was from here that the Special Forces had deployed on the Son Tay rescue mission earlier in the war. I was told to handpick a team from the NTA detachment to train with them. I included myself on the roster.

But while I worked on these new training programs late at night in my little command post at the NTA, it was also apparent that if the worst happened, it would come very quickly and the alert units—our contingency battalions—would deploy very quickly.

For me, it was a time of intense internal conflict.

By now I was over three-quarters of the way through my twelve-month tour and would soon be reassigned back to the States to join Betsy, Tait, and Stuart—both of whom, I knew from the pictures, letters, and occasional phone calls, were growing like weeds.

I wanted to see them again, but what was happening in Vietnam and the possibility that we might well have units going back there was nagging at me. The mood of the whole division reflected the deepening crisis. Lacking the promised American supply support, intelligence, and logistics, whole Vietnamese units were now being overrun. Armed Forces Radio Network News was full of foreboding and the *Stars & Stripes*, the military newspaper for our overseas forces, was looking more and more like it had in 1969 and 1970.

After one of the Sunday afternoon planning conferences at the Division headquarters, I asked to speak with the commander of the 4th Marine Regiment. The 4th Marines were next in the cycle for "Air Alert"—the unit that would be first to deploy in a crisis. I asked him for command of one of the rifle companies in the ready unit. He agreed, and I moved south to Camp Hansen, a base near the center of the island to take command of Company A, 1st Battalion, 4th Marines.

I also did something that I later came to regret as much as anything else I've ever done. I put in a request to extend my tour for several more months. And I wrote home to tell Betsy that I would be missing another Christmas with her and our two children. I was even so rash as to tell her "I know you'll understand, but the new assignment, command of 'A' Company, 1st Battalion, 4th Marines, is very important."

She understood all right. Her response arrived a few weeks later: "I hope you'll stay in touch with the children, but I want a divorce."

Now you might think that a fairly intelligent young fellow who was at least bright enough to graduate from the Naval Academy, get himself through a tour in combat, get "deep selected" to captain, and survive a few other adventures would have said to himself, "We have a problem here. I'd better get home and fix it."

Not I. I told myself that this ungrateful woman really didn't understand what a terrific fella she had married and that I would make everything all right when I finally got home. No matter what she wanted, I was going to extend my stay on Okinawa with my new command, which was about to become the 3d Marine Division's quick reaction force. This was the place to be if there was going to be any U.S. response to the North Vietnamese threat to overrun South Vietnam—and I surely had to be a part of that.

As is so often the case when we think that we're absolutely right about something, I was wrong. The man who was about to take over as my battalion commander, Lieutenant Colonel Chuck Hester, convinced me that extending my tour would be a mistake and that I should go back to the States and try to make things right with my family.

He was a lieutenant colonel and I was only a captain—and I knew how to take a hint. Just before Christmas 1974, I went home expecting that I could quickly repair the marital damage. Once again I was wrong.

Betsy was serious. She really did want a divorce—so I moved into the Quantico Bachelor Officer's Quarters. And that's where our marriage might well have ended—except for a handful of caring comrades. Dick Schulze, the man who had been my battalion commander in Vietnam, and a medical

Vietnam, 1968–1969
Twenty-five years ago, I weighed less.

No one can ever forget the adrenaline rush of a firefight.

Capt. Paul Goodwin (with Capt. Rich O'Neill behind him) made us shave our mustaches, but he also saved a lot of lives.

When you start tossing hand grenades like these Marines are doing along Mutter's Ridge, the enemy is too close.

Helicopters were the lifelines for most soldiers and Marines. They brought supplies and carried out fallen comrades.

They called themselves "Blue Bastards." They weren't mine; I was theirs. I snapped this photo after an operation in "Leatherneck Square."

Defense Department (Marine Corps) and North family collection

I must admit it felt strange to fly into what I remembered as an enemy capital, <u>Hanoi.</u>

Dennis Johnson

Bomb craters are now used as fish ponds (above, top), but transportation is still much the same: <u>bicycle or bus.</u>

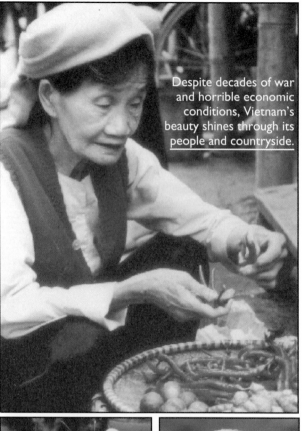

Despite decades of war and horrible economic conditions, Vietnam's beauty shines through its people and countryside.

Outside the walls of the infamous "Hanoi Hilton."

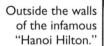

The Vietnamese government lost no time in showing us who won the war. From the military museum in Hanoi (above, top), to the statue celebrating the capture of (now Senator) John McCain (right), to the much photographed remains of a B-52 (above, right), we endured the one-sided history lessons.

Vietnam officially may be a communist nation, but free enterprise flourishes everywhere. Don't bother using the local currency—the dong—or your Visa card. These merchants prefer American dollars.

Some churches, like this dynamic Roman Catholic church in Da Nang, have remained open despite tremendous persecution.

Pastors like Rev. Bui Thu, general secretary of the Evangelical Church of North Vietnam (above), and Father Anthony Nguyen (right) of Da Nang's Roman Catholic Church are real heroes of the Christian faith.

Vietnam's health needs are enormous. Hospitals have only substandard equipment and are forced to reuse disposable syringes and rubber gloves. Dr. Jack Henderson, medical director for the humanitarian agency, International Aid, said this equipment belongs in the Smithsonian. As I toured the hospitals and orphanages and held these precious children, I began to realize that the bandages and antibiotics could allow us to finish what we started in Vietnam.

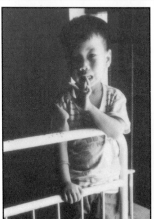

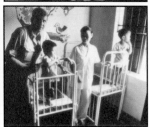

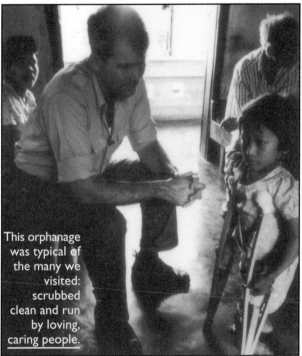

This orphanage was typical of the many we visited: scrubbed clean and run by loving, caring people.

This little guy lost an eye from a Russian-made land mine. Next to malaria, these accidents are the leading cause of death in Vietnam.

Near the old Khe Sanh battlefield, Vietnamese try to eke out a living by cutting wood and scavenging leftover war materials.

The old Khe Sanh runway, scene of Vietnam's longest "siege." To this day, nothing grows on its red latterite soil.

Twenty-five years ago, my platoon held an observation post overlooking Khe Sanh on Hill 950, visible over my right shoulder.

This former NAV officer described how his unit fought against us. Today, we both want to put the war behind us.

One of the most moving moments of my return trip occurred here, at the base of "the Rockpile."

As I recalled the cold and lonely nights I had spent on top of that hill, one of our "guides" came forward and recited the Gettysburg Address.

Not far from the Con Thien firebase, the Vietnamese have their version of Arlington Cemetery—but with no graves or monuments commemorating the fallen soldiers from the South.

IA provides medical support to Vets with a Mission, a group that helps veterans return to help rebuild Vietnam.

IA's medical director, Dr. Jack Henderson, checks tumor growth on this child.

Vets with a Mission

Thanks to Gen. John Vessey, my friends at International Aid resumed their work in Vietnam in 1988. Ralph Plumb, president, couldn't resist giving this lovely orphan a kiss.

I gave "Jefferson cups" to the Vietnamese officials we met and urged them to apply Thomas Jefferson's principles of democracy in Vietnam.

We also enjoyed the hospitality of Col. Jack Donovan (left) who then headed the American task force charged with accounting for all the MIAs. But I'm convinced that ordinary American citizens, like our "ambassador of Polaroid," J. C. Huizenga (below) can also help Vietnam.

With our help and encouragement, one day the people of Vietnam can enjoy real freedom and prosperity.

My return to Vietnam began with a visit to The Wall.

Back home, my fellow officers from the war: (l–r) Art Vandaveer, Ross Petersen, Paul Goodwin, Eric Bowen, Ol' Blue, Rich O'Neill, Jim Lehnert, Bud Flowers, Bill Haskell.

Once again, my best friend and our children kept the home fires burning while I was away: (l–r) Max, Tait, Dornin, Betsy, Stuart, and Sarah.

officer who had been a field surgeon with the Marines in Vietnam finally convinced me to try something that self-made Marines don't care for at all—marriage counseling.

As Larry Boyette, a chaplain at the Quantico Marine Base, helped Betsy and me work through our differences, it became obvious that my plan to stay on Okinawa with the 3d Marine Division wouldn't have made any difference in the outcome of the war. We were still going to marriage counseling as North Vietnamese tanks swept into the South Vietnamese capital. And though Marine helicopters were called in to lift Americans off the roof of our embassy in Saigon, most of the 3d Marine Division remained on Okinawa, waiting for the call to arms that never came.

When Saigon fell, I could not imagine ever being called back to Vietnam. And for nearly twenty years that call didn't come.

PART II
THE RETURN

16

NEW ORDERS

A LITTLE MORE THAN TWO DECADES AFTER I HAD come back from Vietnam, America elected as president a man who, by his own admission, had declined to serve in the war and actively protested against it. Shortly after he was elected, Mr. Clinton announced that he wanted to move toward "normalization" of U.S.-Vietnamese relations. For many, these events were a source of disappointment, anger, and hurt. I must admit to having felt all those emotions.

But as I wrestled with what I felt about Mr. Clinton's presidency and his ideas about our country's relationship with Vietnam, I also found myself digging into a footlocker full of memories, dragging them out, dusting them off, and asking questions about the land I trod over as a young second lieutenant.

My roommate at Basic School had been a South Vietnamese Marine lieutenant, Cao Quang Do. What had happened to him when the South collapsed?

Today what were the old battlefields like that I knew so well—Khe Sanh, Con Thien, Mai Loc, Quang Tri, and others, once ravaged by war? Were they now like other battlefields of other wars, transformed into peaceful countrysides, verdant farmlands, and quaint villages?

Had the attitudes of the Vietnamese people, victorious in the North and defeated in the South, changed toward America? What did the old, dyed-in-the-wool, Ho Chi Minh-style Communists think about the collapse of global communism and the cadaver, once called the Soviet Union?

What about the 2,260 Americans still missing in action in Southeast Asia? Were any still alive? What about the constantly appearing stories of American POWs still being held by the Hanoi government?

Was Vietnam's new "managed market economy" working in one of the world's last five Communist countries? What about the stories of reeducation camps, and political and religious repression?

And what about the accounts, often from refugees, of groups working in Vietnam to provide humanitarian assistance, medical aid, and support for the orphans of the war? Who are these people doing such things, and why were they engaged in such efforts?

I might never have asked myself many of those questions had Bill Clinton not been elected. And I might never have had the chance to return to seek their answers had I not been approached by one of the publishers of my autobiography, *Under Fire*.

At Zondervan, a subsidiary of HarperCollins, publisher Scott Bolinder was working with International Aid, a Michigan-based organization involved in providing medical assistance in Vietnam. From working with me on *Under Fire*, Bolinder knew how strongly I felt about The War and the young men I had served with. He also knew that most of my employees at Guardian Technologies International, the armor company I cofounded in 1989, were refugees from Vietnam.

A week or so before Mr. Clinton's inaugural, Bolinder called. He came right to the point. "What comes to mind first when you think of Vietnam?" he asked.

Without a pause, I replied: "It was such a waste. All those lives."

One of the things I have stopped trying to figure out is why things sometimes work out the way they do. Some people call it luck or coincidence. I call it Divine Providence. I'm convinced that's how Scott Bolinder from Zondervan, Ralph Plumb from International Aid, a Christian humanitarian organization, and I came together.

Scott and Ralph presented a summary of what International Aid had been doing in Vietnam and elsewhere around the world. It was clear that this organization had been able to bring significant help to people in the midst of severe crises. They proposed a trip that would take me back to Vietnam. Its purposes would be straightforward: to allow me to revisit the places I had served and to see what groups like International Aid and others, including many who fought in the Vietnam War, have been doing to help heal the festering wounds of the war.

At first I was skeptical. Most of us who served in Vietnam have packed away our memories of that time and moved on. And even though Mr. Clinton's election had caused many of us to crack open those long-sealed recollections a little, nobody I knew was anxious to air out those dusty recollections again. Most of it was simply too painful.

I also knew that there would be a tremendous amount of apathy, ignorance, and downright hostility to overcome. Most Americans today know little about the area of the world once known as Indochina. A recent survey of high school seniors revealed that fewer than one in five have any idea where the small country that shook the foundations of American society in the 1960s and early '70s is located.

For most Americans over thirty-five, Vietnam is a "syndrome" rather than a place. Vietnam is like a hard-to-shake illness. Its symptoms are, perhaps, increasingly benign. But they plague society nevertheless.

Since our withdrawal in 1975, Vietnam has been portrayed to the American psyche by the twisted images of such "combat films" as *Apocalypse Now*, *Platoon*, *Rambo*, *Born on the Fourth of July*, and more recently and subtly by *Indochine*. The Gulf War may have restored America's pride in its military. But in Vietnam there are still echoes of antiwar demonstrations, body counts, failed presidencies, and a collective national disillusionment that can yet be heard. Besides, I reasoned, everyone is infatuated with how they can become engaged in the former Soviet Union. Nobody cares about the backwater of the former Soviet Union's former colonies, least of all Vietnam.

I told Scott that I would think it over. I had a lot on my plate. I was too busy. I didn't have time.

I was wrong.

A few days later, I had to be in Washington on business. I hate driving into Washington. The traffic is terrible. It gets worse, grows every day. The parking is nonexistent.

As I came across the Roosevelt Memorial Bridge, past the Lincoln Memorial on Constitution Avenue, I noticed that there were open parking spaces along The Mall near the Vietnam Veterans Memorial. Except for inaugurals every four years, January is the slow season for tourists in Washington. The open parking spaces just a few yards from "The Wall" beckoned. I hadn't been here in over a year.

If I had really intended to "just say no" to a return to Vietnam, stopping at the Vietnam Veterans Memorial was a serious mistake. I parked the car and walked across the grass, crisp in the cold air, to the monument. There were no throngs of tourists. They would be here soon enough for the swearing in of a new president, but for now, there was solitude.

From the north, the direction I was coming from, The Wall's black granite, V-shaped surface, is obscured by the terrain. I walked around to the west end, closest to Lincoln, and then down the long, inclined walkway. The polished stone reflected the stars and stripes of the American red-white-and-blue flying above the "three soldiers." On sunny days like this one, the mirror-like surface seems to merge the image of the passerby with the names of the fallen and missing etched in its surface. Inscribed on The Wall is every name of every soldier, sailor, airman, and Marine who was, as the troops used to say, "wasted" in Vietnam. Today there are 58,191 in all, engraved on those stone tablets. The names of the dead appear as they went to and came back from Vietnam: one at a time.

I've been there in that moment when the names that are eternally etched and those whose reflections are fleeting become one on the surface of The Wall. I've seen loved ones brought together once again. I've been there as fallen warriors and standing comrades are rejoined. Nobody can visit that Wall and look at a name, no matter how gray or bright the day, and not have the reflection of the present united to those names engraved from the past. Like almost anyone who has been to The Wall more than once, I've seen real reconciliation and healing take place.

In a very personal way, Vietnam is real at The Wall and the "syndrome" loses some of its debilitating grip. For many, the memorial's utter simplicity begins to heal the complex wounds of a war that, in many ways, is still not over.

I took the long route back to my parked car. *Maybe,* I thought, *I should go back. Maybe now that the cold war is over, it is time to put its battles, both hot and cold, behind us. But that means reconciliation—coming to terms with the past, digging into a "footlocker" full of mixed memories—good, bad, happy, sad—and dealing with what we left behind, what has remained hidden, what we felt too hurt, too angry, sometimes even too betrayed, to deal with before.*

Later that day, I called Bolinder back. "I've thought about this idea for a trip back to Vietnam, and I think there might be some good that can come from it. But I want it to be perfectly clear to anyone involved in this project that I'm not engaged in some kind of phony apology for what I did or what we tried to do in Vietnam. I don't think that's needed or appropriate."

"What do you have in mind?" Scott asked.

"If we can, I'd like to try to reconcile some of the experiences of the past with the realities of the present. I'd also like to deal with the unfinished business of Vietnam. Those of us who went there, whether we came home whole, in pieces, or not at all, never had a chance to complete the mission. Those thoughts struck me pretty hard when I stopped at The Wall today while I was in Washington.

"I want to deal with the one word that keeps haunting me, the word I heard countless times when men were killed. The word that comes to mind every time I go to The Wall. It was the word that came to mind the other day when you first called on this project."

"Which word?" he asked.

"Remember, you asked me 'What comes to mind when you think of Vietnam?'" I responded.

There was a long pause and then Scott said, quietly, "Yes, you said it was 'such a waste.'"

17

GOING BACK

Virginia: April 1993

THE IDEA OF A SMALL TEAM OF FOUR OR FIVE PEOPLE from International Aid and the publisher grew to include a film crew, producer, and a still photographer—fifteen in all. The additional equipment and personnel, and the requirement to schedule time for filming, added a new level of challenge to the venture. After weeks of trying to juggle schedules, itineraries, and deadlines, we set dates for the trip in late April 1993.

Once the dates were decided, I began an intensive course of study—in bureaucracy. First, the visa applications. A ream of forms came in the mail. They had to be submitted in quadruplicate—all originals, please. No carbons, FAXes, or copies

154

allowed. To further complicate the process, all this had to be done through the Vietnamese government offices in Ottawa, Canada.

And then the waiting began. While we waited, we tried to make airline reservations, book hotel rooms, and arrange for meetings and transportation "in-country." Of course, Regulation 47(b), sub-paragraph 13 of the People's Travel Rules (or whatever they're called) required that none of these could be scheduled until our visas, entry and exit permits, and travel documents were issued.

On one of my calls to their embassy in Canada, I asked the very polite government official why we couldn't expedite the process by handling the paperwork through another, cooperating embassy in Washington or even their offices at the United Nations in New York.

She replied, in fluent English, that this was the way things were done, thank you, and did I wish to have any information on the opportunities for investment in Vietnam?

"No, that won't be necessary," I replied. "I'm going to Vietnam with some colleagues to gather information for a book and to shoot some video film for a documentary we are doing about Vietnam."

Maybe it was the word "shoot." Maybe it was the fact that I wasn't interested in investing in Vietnam. Or perhaps it was just that the paperwork included the forms submitted by one very controversial retired Marine. Whatever it was, the processing of our paperwork for the trip seemed to come to a screeching, grinding halt.

Meanwhile, I went about the process of getting the required shots and the like for the trip. And in my effort to find out exactly what shots to get, I made a terrible mistake: I called the Marines!

"You're going where?" asked the incredulous voice at the Marine Headquarters medical clinic.

"Vietnam," I replied.

"Who is this, really?" the voice said.

"This really is Lieutenant Colonel Oliver North, U.S. Marine Corps, Retired," I answered.

"Well, I don't think you can go there. I've never heard of anyone who wants to go there. I mean, who in their right mind wants to go there? Well, now I don't mean it that way, but why on earth would you want to go back there? Besides, I don't even know if we have all the vaccines and things you would need to get shots for. Now let's see, Vietnam, Vietnam . . ."

I could hear this very nice young woman paging through some kind of document. At the rate she was thumbing through the pages, it sounded like a telephone book. And then she started in:

"Here it is, Vietnam: malaria, hepatitis, cholera, typhus, typhoid fever, Japanese encephalitis, diphtheria, tuberculosis, polio, yellow fever, bubonic plague—Lord," she interrupted herself, "did you hear that—bubonic plague!"

Without waiting for comment from me she continued, "melioidosis, parasites, internal and external, rabies, tropical sprue, leprosy. Leprosy!?" She interrupted herself again. "Are you sure you want to go back there?"

Before she could continue the litany, I assured her that I really was going back to Vietnam and thanked her for the information. She offered to put me in touch with a Navy medical officer to see how many inoculations were required, but I decided that would simply invite another inquisition about why I would be considering such a trip.

Instead of visiting the Navy clinic for what sounded to me like several thousand injections, I called a civilian doctor I knew down the road to see what was really required. Dr. Parry called back in less than an hour:

"You know, the Immigration and U.S. Public Health people no longer require anything for readmittance to the United States, but I would suggest that you want to get something for typhus, some gamma globulin for the hepatitis and plague, and a cycle of anti-malarial medication. Since your tetanus is up to date, the only one that requires you to come in is the gamma globulin. All the rest are pills that you take on a specific schedule."

Finally some good news! The fact that only one shot was required was within the limits of my basic cowardice when it comes to doctors and dentists. I made the appointment.

As our April departure date approached, we still had no paperwork that would allow us to get on the flight that would take us from the U.S. to Vietnam and return. On the promise from the Vietnam embassy in Ottawa that the paperwork really would arrive on time, Ralph Plumb dispatched Joel Samy, who was then one of his deputies at International Aid and the planner of the trip, to make the requisite arrangements for our travel once we got to Vietnam. Back home, we made our reservations: Washington to Chicago, to Tokyo, to Bangkok, to Hanoi, Vietnam. In all, twenty-four hours in airplanes and airports. Ah, the marvels of modern travel!

By mid-April as our departure date approached, I'd decided that there was very little that could happen that would make this trip any more complicated. As usual, I was wrong.

We weren't exactly trying to keep our venture a secret, but all involved believed that a low-profile trip without a lot of press attention would be more conducive to the kind of work we wanted to do and the places we wanted to visit. By then it was also clear that our hosts were more comfortable with this kind of visit. We all thought we could keep it that way. There were no big stories coming out of Vietnam. The flurry of press created by Mr. Clinton's suggestions about normalization had faded.

Sounded great. No press, no reporters, no "newsies" hanging around. It seemed almost too good to be true. It was.

I should have known better. I am, after all, the author of North's third corollary to Murphy's law: "Nothing is ever as easy as it ought to be." That much I was right about.

Just days before boarding the plane that would take me back to Southeast Asia, I was sitting with my mouth cranked all the way open, listening to the radio while Dr. Bobby Sears, our family dentist, replaced a loose filling in one of my molars.

"Unless you're going to write about the dental care over there, you probably ought to let me fix that before you go," he'd said. Usually, it takes me six months to a year to get around to making a dental appointment after a check-up. This time I was in his office the next day.

He was drilling out the old filling when the news came on. The lead story went something like this:

Vietnamese officials today called a document bogus that claims 600 more American POWs were held by Hanoi than previously have been claimed. The memo, found in Moscow by a Harvard University researcher, raises new questions about Communist Vietnam's. . . .

I must have started because Bobby stopped drilling and asked, "Did that hurt?"

"No, not you, but that story sure does," I replied. "If that's true, I don't want to have anything to do with those people."

"Well, how will you know if you don't go and find out for yourself?" Bobby said. "You, of all people know that you can't believe the press." It's nice to have a dentist who is both a good tooth fixer and a friend.

When I got out of the dentist's chair and back to my office, I set out to find out all I could about the news report. With help from Senator John McCain's office and Senator Bob Smith, I was able to collect enough essential information to reassure me about the trip.

John McCain, U.S. Naval Academy class of 1956, had spent more than six years as a prisoner of the North Vietnamese. Injured when he ejected from his badly damaged Navy jet over North Vietnam, he had suffered terribly from inadequate medical treatment and the brutality of some of his captors.

As a U.S. congressman and senator from Arizona he had been actively engaged in the issue of American POWs and MIAs for more than a decade.

Senator Bob Smith from New Hampshire is also a veteran of Vietnam. He, too, had served in Vietnam, in the Gulf of Tonkin, and like his colleague, John McCain, took an active interest in efforts to determine the fate of those Americans who had gone to Vietnam but never returned.

Both men had been back to Vietnam several times and both maintained a healthy skepticism about all that they were told. I knew that both had been part of the Senate Select Committee on POW/MIA Affairs and had strong feelings about the new administration's plans for "normalization" with Vietnam before we had all the answers about what had happened to our missing men.

I expressed my concerns that my visit not get caught up in the political wrangling over this new revelation. Both said that they understood and encouraged me to press on with our trip. Senator McCain gave me a letter of introduction to help open some doors for us in Vietnam, and Senator Smith called to offer some last-minute counsel on how to avoid being used by the various factions vying for influence and access. Both proved to be valuable.

Even with this last-minute input and advice, it appeared that our hope for a quiet trip without controversy was now out of the question. Vietnam was once again the center of attention for the American media.

The document found in the Soviet military intelligence archives in Moscow certainly warranted the stories it generated. Reputable experts described it as a Russian translation of an internal North Vietnamese Army report to the Vietnamese Politburo from General Tran Van Quang, who was identified in the document as the deputy chief of staff of the North Vietnamese Army. Its contents described efforts to keep secret the true number of Americans being held prisoner by the North Vietnamese. At that time Vietnam acknowledged holding 368. The newly found report said that 1,205 U.S. servicemen were prisoners.

In addition to the explosive nature of the information, there were several other things about the report that I found to be fascinating. First, it was clear that, at least in 1972, the Soviets were spying on their erstwhile allies. And second, notwithstanding all the "warming" of relations between Washington and Moscow under the Gorbachev regime, it had taken the election of Boris Yeltsin, Moscow's former mayor, to bring information like this to the light of day.

But I was headed for Hanoi, not Moscow, and this new revelation was clearly complicating the prospects for a successful trip. The news was a bombshell to the new administration quietly planning a rapprochement with the Vietnamese government. The newspapers and news broadcasts were full of accusations of Hanoi's duplicity.

Angry veterans' groups, families of the missing, and many ordinary citizens, joined the outcry for an immediate reckoning from the Hanoi government. Senator McCain and a small congressional delegation went to Hanoi and the Clinton Administration dispatched a man of unquestioned integrity, retired U.S. Army General John "Jack" Vessey, a hero of WWII, Korea, and Vietnam, one of America's most decorated soldiers, and the former Chairman of the Joint Chiefs of Staff.

Since shortly after his retirement in 1985, General Vessey had served as three presidents' representative to the Hanoi government on POW/MIA matters. President Reagan had asked him to take on this task and his mandate had been renewed by President Bush. Now, according to press reports, Mr. Clinton was sending him once again to Hanoi to determine the validity of the information in what everyone recognized to be an authentic Soviet document.

In the seven years he had been engaged in this painful task, General Vessey had been able to make some progress, though much of it came slowly, seemingly an inch at a time.

Thanks to General Vessey and the families of the men still missing, Congress had provided funds to establish a small American base dedicated to "full accounting," within the Hanoi city limits. Its staff of elite specialists were given virtual carte blanche to visit remote locations where remains of Americans might be found or "live sightings" had reportedly taken place.

Though we had long planned a visit to the U.S. Task Force – Full Accounting, I did not want our visit to generate speculation that this was the only purpose of our trip. None of us could have anticipated this last-minute turn of events and there was no way for us to rearrange our schedule. Thankfully, a call to General Vessey's office at the Pentagon confirmed that our paths would not cross and we would not interfere with his mission. As promised, the officers and NCOs we talked to did not divulge our travel plans. Further, they informed us, contrary to speculation in the media, that General Vessey's upcoming trip to Vietnam had, like ours, been routinely planned well before the recent revelations though he would be taking up the matter of the "Soviet document" in the course of his regular meetings with the officials in Hanoi.

Best of all, they told us, General Vessey would not be arriving in Vietnam until several days after we did. If things worked out as we hoped, we could get into and out of Hanoi before the press pool covering the Vessey visit even arrived.

It almost worked. Only a small handful of the local "Hanoi press corps" spotted us, and thanks to some quick work by writer David Roth, they restrained themselves from reporting that "Oliver North was in Hanoi in violation of the Logan Act conducting a covert operation to free captives held by Communists."

Like so many other things in life, things that appeared very difficult and worrisome at the time turned out for the best. Reflecting on all the roadblocks and obstacles that seemed to arise in the course of getting to Vietnam, it was, after all, well worth the effort to overcome them. And while they did not seem so at the time, some of the events that occurred turned out to be downright humorous.

One of those "funny little things that happened on my way to Hanoi" was of my own making.

Well before the idea of a trip to Vietnam had even been suggested, I had agreed to host the Rush Limbaugh radio show for him while he was on vacation. And before we set the dates for the journey, Rush and I had agreed that I would do the show on April 5, 6, and 7. As it turned out, that was just prior to our departure for Vietnam.

One afternoon during the show, my mother called the studio and the guys in the control room who turn the dials and make the show work decided to play a gag on their harried "guest host." Just before the end of that day's show they signaled me to take one last call from "Jane, in New York City." Of course that's not my mother's name nor where she lives.

I did as asked and said into the microphone: "Jane, in New York City, you're live on the air—what's on your mind?"

The next thing I hear is a voice I've known for nearly fifty years, asking something about what was going to be done to rebuild America's crumbling infrastructure.

"Mom? Mom, is that you?" I asked, forgetting that we were broadcasting to millions of radios.

"Yes, dear, it's me. I just thought I'd call to see how you're doing on the radio."

I couldn't believe it. I looked up to see Peter, the engineer behind the large soundproof glass, doubled up in laughter.

"Mom, we're live, on the air, broadcasting. Do you know that?"

"Yes, dear," she replied. "I really just called to find out if you were going to come to see me on my birthday."

"Mom, there are millions of people listening to this conversation. Do you want to tell all America how old you're going to be?"

"Certainly, dear, I'll be seventy-five!" she said proudly. And then: "You are coming, aren't you?"

My brothers and sister and I had been secretly planning a surprise party for her anyway, but there was no point in trying to explain all this on a live broadcast. "Sure, Mom, I'll be there."

As soon as the show was over, I called her back. "Mom, why did you do that?" I asked.

"Well, dear, I knew you wouldn't turn me down in front of all those people." Ah, how well our mothers know us!

If I'd ever had any doubts about the reach and range of the Rush Limbaugh show, they were dispelled a few days later when we were rushing through the airport in Bangkok, Thailand. From well down the terminal a voice with a distinctly American accent shouted: "Hey, Ollie! Ollie! Over here!"

I looked to see a man in a U.S. Army uniform. He waved and shouted again: "Hey, Ollie, did you go to your Mom's birthday?"

The crowd around erupted in laughter. Did everybody in the world know? "Not yet," I shouted back, "but I will."

And so I did. We returned from Vietnam just in time for my brothers, sister, and me to gather at Mom's apartment for her seventy-fifth. It made a nice capstone to our adventure in Vietnam. But that's another story.

Despite all the revelations and "hot" news out of Washington and Hanoi, our departure in 1993 was, in the end, remarkably similar to the one I had made twenty-five years earlier. It was noted only by our families and a few close friends who said a prayer that our travels would be safe and our return timely. Thankfully, that part worked the way it was supposed to.

18

GETTING THINGS DONE

Hanoi, Vietnam: April 1993

I'M REMINDED OF THAT OLD ADVERTISING SLOGAN "Getting there is half the fun!" Well if that's true, then the other "half the fun" is trying to invent new ways of getting things done once you're there. One of the few sad things about the passing of communism is that our children won't have the chance to see *real* bureaucrats in action. I've never been much of a fan of bureaucrats in any government, but try as they may, our federal apparatchiks are pikers compared to those in Communist regimes. In Communist countries, even those few that are left, bureaucrats take the words RED TAPE very seriously. For Communists, it's part of the culture.

But for the Vietnamese people, a basic civility and

hospitable demeanor are also part of the culture. And so, the desire to be a good party bureaucrat often finds itself in direct conflict with the innate desire of the typical Vietnamese to be a gracious host.

Thankfully, the latter won out over the former and we were offered a genuinely warm welcome when we arrived in Hanoi. Because of the credibility and connections that International Aid had carefully built and cultivated since it first started its medical relief work in Vietnam in 1988, we were given special status by the Ministry of Health. A car met us at the Air France 747 we'd flown in from Bangkok to Hanoi, and we breezed through customs, directly to a pleasant reception in an air-conditioned lounge next to the main terminal.

After our baggage arrived, we piled into three large vans for the forty-minute trip to downtown Hanoi. Immediately upon leaving the airport it became obvious that we were in a country that was suffering severely.

Here at home we're used to hearing complaints about the "crumbling infrastructure" of America's cities. Those who want to grouse about the potholes in Washington, D.C.'s city streets ought to visit some of the rest of the world's capitals. Many, like Hanoi, have no worry about potholes in the paving. On much of the main road from the airport into the city there is no paving!

In the last thirty years of my life I've been blessed to be able to travel in Europe, the Middle East, Latin America, Africa, and of course, the "Orient." One thing I've learned in those travels is not to make snap judgments about a place based only on what you see—and certainly not what you see on the way into the capital city from the airport.

But I've also learned that some of those first impressions can be lasting, no matter how much you tell yourself that they shouldn't be. And after all, I reminded myself, these aren't my "first impressions." I spent a whole year in this country. So I guess these are my "second impressions":

1. Baseball Hats. Vietnam has more baseball hats than I've ever seen in my life. It is part of the standard uniform for every child old enough to walk and much of the adult population as well. In much of the country the baseball hat has replaced the non, the traditional straw conical hat that used to typify this part of the world. These baseball hats, I noticed, were emblazoned with the name of every major-league team in America. But corporate America was equally well represented: "CAT," "John Deere," "Texaco," "Marlboro," and "Bush Hog," were among the most obvious. I wondered if there was an active black market for certain teams, or names that were more valuable than others. When I asked one of our government-provided "guides" about this, he just shrugged. But I didn't trust him anyway. He was wearing a black Oakland Raiders hat. I'm a Redskins fan.

2. Bicycles. There must be at least three bicycles for every human being in Vietnam. And they are used to carry everything. A short list of things we saw being transported on bicycles: people (as many as three), pigs, dogs, chickens, steel pipe, bricks, bags of cement, rice, water, gasoline, truck tires, chairs, roofing tiles—the list is endless. When I was here twenty-five years before, we had triggered an ambush

on what we thought was an NVA patrol moving down a trail along the edge of the Laotian border. It turned out to be a group of NVA soldiers on heavily laden bicycles, loaded down with weapons, ammunition, and equipment for their comrades farther south. The bicycle is still the universal means of transportation in Vietnam. Somewhere, there is probably a statue to their greatest bike builder. If there isn't, there ought to be.

3. New Construction. The entire country is being rebuilt. There is no structure of any kind—large, small, residential, commercial, government, rural, urban, primitive, or sophisticated that is not under construction, renovation, or restoration. The building program was so obvious and so pervasive that I asked if there was some kind of law that required every structure with a roof to continuously be having some kind of work done on it. Once again I was treated to a shrug. Whether there is such a law or not, the extraordinary amount of construction ongoing throughout the length of the country is one of the most obvious indicators of the incredible resourcefulness and energy of these people.

4. Crumbling Soviet-made Junk. Broken-down Soviet trucks, tractors, road graders, helicopters, transport aircraft, and machinery of every possible type and purpose is in evidence everywhere. It would appear that almost nothing the Russians brought to Vietnam still works. The great triumph of scientific socialism seemed to be a one cylinder, two-wheeled garden-type tractor that makes a poor substitute for a bicycle on some back roads. Not any were seen to be doing any cultivating or farm work, but some enterprising entrepreneurs were

obviously using them for delivery services. One of the most painfully visible reminders of the Soviet role in Vietnam is the remarkable number of edifices they had constructed throughout the country. The architecture is in the modern socialist motif; grand, gaudy, larger than life, and almost totally useless. The Russians had also perfected a certain technique that made the buildings they constructed truly unique. Using a process known only to them, the concrete they had poured as recently as three or four years ago all appeared to be at least a century or two old. Thus, these relatively new structures, with their crumbling facades, faded frescoes, and mismatched hues all appeared to pre-date the Ming dynasty. These structures may well have contributed to the outbreak of new construction, noted above.

5. The Smiles. Notwithstanding all of the other impressions I shall retain of this trip to Vietnam, there is one that is paramount: the almost universal smile that greeted us everywhere we went. Now a smile is something special. Perhaps not in a diplomat or government official. That's their job. They are supposed to smile and make people, particularly visiting firemen, believe that they are welcome and the like, even when they're not. But from the average man or woman on the street, it's something different. A smile that comes spontaneously to the lips of a stranger who suddenly encounters you in a place you're not expected isn't something that can be scripted by a commissar or a block warden, even in a police state. And in Vietnam, the reflexive smiles were all the broader, all the more visibly heartfelt, the moment a person we encountered discovered that we were Americans. This was an intriguing

experience for me—and it happened everywhere throughout the country. I had expected those who lived in the north, particularly around Hanoi, to have bitter memories of our bombing raids during the war. And in the south, I thought that there would be resentment because we had abandoned them. Yet when we met the average man, woman, or child on the street and they ascertained that we were Americans, a candid, unrehearsed smile would burst forth, almost instinctively, like a new sunrise. These smiles came unconsciously, in cities, in the countryside, in hospitals, from wounded, disabled veterans from both sides, from parents and children, farmers, merchants, young and old. The smiles of the people of Vietnam will be the most indelible memory I keep from my return there.

There is another memory I shall retain from our 1993 trip to Vietnam, and that pertains to the very formal method by which visitors sometimes can cut through the official "RED TAPE." But first, a disclaimer. By including this passage in this book I do not wish to suggest to any reader that I, in any way, endorse the methods I am about to describe. Secondly, please note that the names of various officials of the government of Vietnam have been changed to protect the guilty. I am simply recounting this particular tale so that unwary visitors in the future will not be taken advantage of by the unscrupulous. And while no good, God-fearing believer would dare to condone or participate in the practice described below, it is always helpful to know how others get things done in a Communist system. It's kind of like carrying a spare tire in your car. You never want to use it, but it's nice to know it's there.

In a country with a transportation and communications network as disrupted as that in Vietnam it is inevitable that changes will occur in the planned itinerary. Once this occurs, you can expect that the most routine of requests will be met with a perfunctory: "No, we cannot do that."

At this point there is a ritual procedure that must be pursued all the way to conclusion, or you can expect all of your subsequent plans to fall awry. The process can best be likened to a formal Asian dance—at the end of which, the request is granted.

Based on reports from seasoned travelers in Vietnam, here is a scenario that will describe the process. I cannot personally vouch for its effectiveness since I never tried it:

"Mr. Trung, tomorrow, instead of visiting the western part of your country, we ought to drive north so that we can visit some of your rural villages," someone asked.

"No," said Trung, "we cannot do that."

At this point the left hand must be inserted in the pocket where Mr. Trung by now knows you keep your U.S. dollars. His eyes will follow the movement carefully. Then, according to the ritual, Mr. Trung will say, "Well, I may be able to do something, but it will be very difficult."

Now it is incumbent on the part of the requester to sympathize with the beleaguered guide, while removing several bills from said left pocket. "Yes, I'm sure it is very hard to do, but you are very expert at these things, Mr. Trung."

"Well, perhaps something can be worked out, but I must be able to cover the extraordinary expenses that we will incur."

The expected reply is, of course, to sympathize further, but not so much as to incur unnecessary expense. "What do you think the expenses will be, Mr. Trung?"

"Well, about $50, I should guess." This of course means a split of unknown proportions between Mr. Trung and the others to whom he must talk. It is expected that this declaration of amount will be met with a whoosh of air from the mouth of the harried "tourist."

The "tourist" must now present Mr. Trung with an amount, at least twenty percent less than that requested, along with a plaintive request that he "please, see if this will be enough," while pressing two folded $20 bills into his hand. At this point, it is important that the tourist look as if he has absolutely no more money and is prepared to walk away if he cannot be helped.

Mr. Trung is now obliged to look deeply dismayed at this paltry amount and say something to the effect that "these things are very difficult to do . . ." as he exits, shaking his head, toward the door.

Protocol demands that Mr. Trung (or your "guide") remain out of sight until at least a half hour past the absolute latest that you have told him you had to have an answer. He also must reappear by bursting into whatever meeting you happen to be in, covered with sweat but grinning from ear to ear as if he has just witnessed a miracle at his own hand.

Formality demands that Mr. Trung now expound

at great length on the heroic victory he has just won over Communist red tape, the bureaucratic hurdles he has leaped, and the harrowing escape he has engineered for you from the reeducation camps into which you were about to be cast for daring to deviate from the officially published itinerary.

It would, of course, be too crude and impolitic to refer to this process as bribery, graft, or official corruption, so we quickly developed a phrase for it—the "Bonus Incentive Plan" (B.I.P.).

19

THOSE WE LEFT BEHIND

Hanoi, Vietnam: April 1993

SINCE WE WERE GUESTS OF THE MINISTRY OF Health, one of the agency's officials had arranged for our team to stay at the nicest hotel in Hanoi. Any concerns I might have had that we would stand out like large Anglo-Saxon sore thumbs were immediately dispelled. Hanoi in general, and this hotel in particular, was bustling with businessmen, all trying to break into the enormous market that Vietnam's nearly seventy million people represents. British, Australian, French, German, Dutch, Indonesian, Malaysian, Taiwanese, and Japanese businessmen bustled through the lobbies, filled the elevators, and crowded into the restaurants at mealtimes. Apparently Hanoi is no longer on the regular tourist route for Russian travelers, since they were about the only nationality we didn't identify.

As protocol demanded, our first meetings were with our hosts at the Ministry of Health. Housed in a great, yellow, French Colonial-era building in the government sector of the city, surrounded by stately trees, I felt as though we had just stepped back into the 1940s.

Despite the considerable size of our delegation, we were formally and very cordially welcomed by Vietnam's Minister of Health, Dr. Nguyen Trong Nhan, and his staff in an attractively appointed, high-ceilinged conference room. The green-shuttered windows and slowly rotating fans completed the illusion of having stepped into a time warp. The only dead giveaway that we were still in 1993 was the brand-new Panasonic air conditioner humming quietly and with welcome effect in one of the windows.

Ralph Plumb, president of International Aid, introduced our party and described our itinerary. Dr. Nhan made several comments about our ambitious schedule, suggested some ways in which we could maximize the use of our available time, and offered to be of any assistance. Then, when it appeared to me that the meeting was about to conclude, Dr. Nhan turned to me and in perfect English said, "So, Colonel, what do you think of this paper that has supposedly just been found in Moscow?"

The way he asked the question left no doubt in my mind as to what document he was referring to and how he felt about it. And while I did not want to start our trip on a note that could well make the rest of our stay unpleasant, I thought he deserved a straightforward answer.

"I think the document raises some very serious questions. As you know, Dr. Nhan, many Americans, including those of us in this room, feel very strongly about the need for a full accounting of those who did not return from the war."

He listened as the interpreter translated, and then replied, "Yes, I know, we are cooperating with your government on this matter, but this document from Moscow is not authentic."

His statement was made without rancor or hostility, but it was clear that he wanted to make his point. So did I.

"I have not seen the document and I am not an expert in such things, but I have been led to believe that the document itself is indeed authentic. Apparently the question is whether or not the information it contains is accurate."

"Yes, quite. Well I can assure you that it is not. I hope that it does not create another obstacle to normalization." With that, and a series of friendly handshakes, the meeting ended, and we were courteously escorted back to our vehicles. That meeting was simply the first of many similar sessions we would have in Vietnam. And like every other meeting, it was cordial, formal, and addressed two very specific issues: the "Moscow Document," and "normalization" of U.S.-Vietnamese diplomatic and economic relationships. There was never any doubt how our hosts felt about these two matters: The contents of the "Moscow Document" were simply bogus, and "normalization" was absolutely essential.

By the time I returned from Vietnam, I'd had quite my fill of both issues and decided that each was considerably overblown by almost all concerned.

Though the whole story may never be known, the infamous "Moscow Document" appears to be what its finder, Stephen Morris, claims—a 1972 Soviet military intelligence document, seemingly based upon a Vietnamese original. But after that, little is certain. There are sufficient historical and other irrefutable, factual inaccuracies in it to raise questions about just how accurate the Soviet intelligence services really were. How the document was created, why it was created, and by whom, remains unclear.

In the end, the document proved to be of no help in answering questions about the fate of the Americans who remain unaccounted for. Instead it reopened painful wounds and stirred hopes that remain unfulfilled. Our hosts were right about one thing, however; the document did throw very cold water on the talk of early normalization of relations.

That word *normalization* hangs over every conversation in Vietnam. Hotel clerks, government apparatchiks, old retired veterans on *both* sides—all talk of "normalization" as though it is the Great Panacea. You can almost hear the chants: "Normalization will solve all our problems."

There is no doubt that it will have some positive benefits for the Vietnamese, but unless their government creates real protection for private property and encourages private capital investment, the effects are likely to be negligible. Nearly every other country on earth is already there anyway. The Japanese are building power grids. The Germans are building telecommunications. The French are building roads and bridges.

What do they want from the Americans? Trade, investment, loans, recognition, of course. But there is more to it than just American money or technology. I returned home with the sense that the people of Vietnam—as distinguished from the government of Vietnam—genuinely like Americans and sincerely want to put the past behind them.

Yet, despite the evident goodwill of the Vietnamese people toward Americans, significant obstacles remain in addition to the POW/MIA issue. The U.S. has not had diplomatic relations with Vietnam since The War and has publicly declared that normalization will not occur until all Vietnamese troops are withdrawn from neighboring Cambodia (Kampuchea) and the Cambodians have held free elections leading to the formation of a new government. U.N.-monitored elections were held there in the spring of 1993, shortly after our visit, but the results have been contested by the various factions vying for power.

Others are opposed to "normalization" until internal political and religious freedoms are assured in Vietnam. Critics point to continuing human rights abuses, political repression, and efforts by the Hanoi government to keep both the Christian and Buddhist religious communities from flourishing.

But as contentious as these matters are, the most volatile issue is the final resolution of American POWs and MIAs. It is the one factor today that transfixes American thinking on Vietnam, the one issue that has galvanized otherwise disparate persons and groups in opposition to "normalization."

America's focus on the POW/MIA issue explains why something like the Moscow archive document can so readily grip America's attention and so freely twist our emotions.

Since returning from my April '93 trip I must have been asked 500 times: "Do you think there are any POWs still being held?" and by others, "What's being done about the MIAs; will we ever find them all?"

I can honestly say that I don't know whether any Americans are still being held. I do know that every possible effort is being made by our government to find out what happened to those who are missing and unaccounted for. And I believe that those involved in that effort are dedicated men and women of integrity and resourcefulness. But that does not mean that we will ever have all the answers for every case. Nor does it mean that the answers they find will satisfy every American or every group that has expressed concern over the fate of missing Americans.

Some will always believe that American prisoners and the remains of others were—and are—being held by the Vietnamese government as leverage or "bargaining chips" for dealing with the U.S. government. There are those who believe that this has been an ongoing policy of Hanoi's ever since the U.S. failed to deliver the more than $3 billion in post-war reconstruction aid promised as part of the 1973 Paris peace accords.

Ten years before I worked for him at the National Security Council in the Reagan Administration, Robert C. "Bud" McFarlane, then an assistant to Dr. Henry Kissinger, was dispatched to offer Hanoi

$100 million in medical and humanitarian aid in return for any prisoners remaining after 577 American POWs were repatriated in Operation Homecoming. No American airmen shot down over Laos were among this group.

And, if these facts of history are not troubling enough, to further complicate America's difficult reckoning and resolution of this issue, "live sighting reports" persist to this day. Some, like former Marine Robert Garwood who was convicted in 1979 of collaborating with the enemy, are regarded to be less than credible. But others, to include reports from Vietnamese and Laotian refugees, have a ring of truth to them though none has ever been confirmed.

Tragically, reports such as these generate waves of false hope in the hearts and minds of those who wait for word—any word—of loved ones long lost but never confirmed deceased. Perhaps worst of all are the extortionists and soldiers of fortune who, bearing phony photographs or dog tags, promise, for a fee, to bring home the long-awaited warrior, ostensibly held hostage, or in other cases, the remains of a dead husband, father, or son. In numerous cases, grieving relatives have given thousands of dollars to such charlatans. None of them has produced the promised results. All have added to the heartache already borne by the families of the missing.

To help families of the missing cope with the falsehoods, anxiety, and sometimes seeming intransigence of their own government, a group of POW/MIA wives decided to organize to support one another and, to the extent they could, help their men in bondage. Initially headed by Sybil Stockdale, the wife of Navy flyer James Stockdale, the group eventually incorporated as a nonprofit foundation in 1970. Today, the National League of Families of American Prisoners and Missing in Southeast Asia has over 3,500 members nationwide. These brave women actively campaigned to make the world aware of the brutal treatment their men were receiving long before Operation Homecoming. After the releases in 1973, those who did come home confirmed that their treatment improved as a consequence of the League's work.

But nearly 2,300 men remain unaccounted for, and because progress in finding remains and resolving reports is so painstakingly slow, every organization involved, the League of Families and the U.S. government included, has been subjected to criticism. Conspiracy theories, "cover-up" stories, and accusations abound. Sadly, none of this has helped advance the resolution of what has happened to the missing Americans.

On our last night in Hanoi, we went to the compound where the U.S. Task Force – Full Accounting is headquartered. Here is a U.S. military installation, which routinely dispatches crash-site investigation units deep within the country's interior, located in the capital city of a nation with which we have no diplomatic relations. At the time we were there, U.S. Army Lieutenant Colonel Jack Donovan headed the team, and he graciously held an American-style cook-out for us (complete with hamburger flown in from Bangkok), though he was also in the midst of preparing for General Vessey's visit the following day.

I asked Colonel Donovan and his team of Army, Air Force, Navy, and Marine experts the same question that we would be asked countless times on our return: "Are there any Americans still being held against their will?"

The team's universal opinion was, "No." They did not believe that the Hanoi government was holding any live Americans, although they willingly admitted that they could not prove it and that it was entirely possible that in the hinterlands, or in Laos, some Americans could be held by "warlords" outside the control of the government.

I was impressed with Donovan's team and his leadership. Many of his team were veterans of the war, and now they were back in Vietnam carrying out the slow, diligent, painstaking work that was leading to the location of remains—usually very partial, fragmentary ones. They were using the best equipment and methods available to locate, recover, and identify their countrymen. Often the teams would have to hike for days to get to a crash site, carrying on their backs all their equipment, food, and shelter—just as we had done two decades before.

Yet, even as their difficult work progressed, these men and women, too, had felt the sting of criticism from those who thought the pace of resolution too slow, and the cooperation of Vietnamese officials was too sporadic.

When I got back home, I was able to read some of the reports to Congress on the effectiveness of the Task Force. And matching those reports with what we saw in Vietnam, it is possible to draw some very interesting conclusions:

- First, the cooperation of the Vietnamese government with our effort to locate, recover, and identify American remains has slowly but steadily improved since it began with a visit in 1982 by Deputy Assistant Secretary of Defense Richard Armitage. Rich, a classmate of mine from Annapolis, had started this ball rolling.
- Second, the average Vietnamese is more than a little baffled about the American focus on this issue. Their puzzlement is the consequence of the dramatic differences between their culture and ours, and one very stark fact: The people of Vietnam still cannot account for more than 300,000 of their own sons and daughters lost, on both sides, in war between 1960 – 75.
- Third, for those of us who have trudged through the mountainous triple-canopied jungle, such a number is not surprising. What I find to be more astonishing is that the number of Americans missing or unaccounted for is as low as it is. Much of Vietnam's lush foliage is so dense that entering it is like being devoured by nature. Given the severity of much of the terrain, the humid tropical climate, the animals of the wild, and the sparse population outside the country's towns and cities, it is a tribute to American bravery and persistence that the number isn't much higher.

In all, counting the confirmed dead and MIAs, the United States lost more than 60,000 of its sons and daughters in Southeast Asia. Because battlefield search and rescue technology had significantly improved, and medevac capabilities had advanced, it was possible to retrieve the bodies of more than 95 percent of all those who fell in Vietnam. This far surpasses the tally for other modern conflicts. Nearly three times as many Americans never returned from Korea and 78,794 of those who served in World War II remain unaccounted for.

Those numbers from other wars, of course, do nothing to assuage the lingering pain, sadness, emptiness, and anger felt by those who sent a loved one off to war who never returned. But even though we who served in Vietnam did a better job of returning the remains of our fallen comrades-in-arms than in any prior war, the issue has ignited stronger passions in Vietnam than any other modern war. Why?

Some say that the collective attention, frustration, grief, and anger over Americans missing in action are the consequence of special interest groups such as the League of Families, the Vietnam Veterans of America (VVA), or former Navy POW "Red" McDaniel's American Defense Institute and their public affairs programs. I disagree. While I believe that these groups have been helpful in supporting the families of the missing, they could not have unilaterally created the conditions necessary to sustain the focus of the American people on this issue.

In the nearly two decades since the end of the war, the POWs and MIAs have come to symbolize American sentiment about the Vietnam war. The black POW/MIA banner with its white silhouette of an American POW in a barbed-wire enclosure and a guard tower is now commonplace in schools, churches, parades, and civic functions across America. It is the smaller version of this logo, worn as a patch, that one sees on so many of the camouflage-clad vets on America's city streets. The kind of deep regard Americans display toward our POWs and MIAs reflects a preexisting emotional attachment to this issue. Why does this issue captivate us as it does?

It may well be that for many Americans, veterans and others, the POWs/MIAs have become the one issue that unites us all about The War. By the late 1960s, the turmoil and confusion over American involvement in Vietnam led to a national condition of ambivalence. When those who served did not come home as they had fought—in squads, platoons, companies, and battalions, but alone, one-by-one, occasionally harassed, sometimes scorned, but mostly unnoticed—the issue of Vietnam remained unsettled. The only ones who came home to a heroes' welcome were the POWs who returned together, as a group. Painful as it may be to acknowledge, deep inside themselves the American people know that as a nation we didn't treat the other Vietnam vets right—those who answered the call to service, whether eagerly or reluctantly, and served faithfully—those who did their duty and came home again after their one-year tours.

Among many who were adults back then, there is a nagging sense of collective guilt. Few really want to accept that we lost. And because guilt, valid or not, interferes with the ability to move on, we cannot seem to entirely close the door and put The War behind us. We did not carry to its conclusion the mission on which we embarked, and we did not stand squarely behind the young men and women who fought. As a nation we abandoned and rejected our countrymen who had served on the battle-field when they returned singly from that failed task. Now, years later, it is easier for us to assuage the guilt from those days so long ago by harboring hatred toward the captors of those we saw collectively as heroes—the POWs, and by association, the MIAs.

Ultimately, anger of this sort is destructive. It prevents us from getting beyond where we are today. The wisdom of the Bible instructs us to reconcile with our enemies—a great teaching but tough to practice. But as one who has looked the enemy in the eye both in the battlefield and then in his own devastated country, I believe that reconciliation can happen—not through the kind of government-to-government "normalization" being talked about in Hanoi and Washington but through a more creative avenue.

When General Vessey returned from his first trip to Hanoi in mid-1987, he started the process of opening the door for nongovernmental humanitarian relief organizations to be admitted to Vietnam. In the agreement worked out at the time, it was understood by both Washington and Hanoi that U.S. humanitarian-relief organizations could proceed to ". . . address humanitarian concerns and not link them to broader political issues such as normalization of diplomatic relations, resumption of trade, or economic aid."

General Vessey's formula, developed by an aging warrior but grounded in the solid Judeo-Christian teaching about clothing the naked and feeding the hungry, has provided us with an opportunity to complete the mission we failed to finish as a nation.

By actively engaging in providing help, directly from one people to another, outside the framework of government, we also have the occasion to honor those who served in Vietnam, whether alive or dead, well or maimed, home or not.

20

COMMUNISM THEN AND NOW

Vietnam: 1968, 1973

LIKE MANY OTHER "PROFESSIONAL SOLDIERS" IN OUR nation's Armed Forces, I spent much of my life deeply involved with the struggle against communism. Though I was born in the midst of the great world war against totalitarian fascism, it was communism that was our one great recognized enemy from the time I was a schoolchild to the beginning of this decade. As young man at Annapolis we studied it, as we did in every military course I attended thereafter. My colleagues and I, professional military officers, carefully digested everything we could about communism's many guises, insidious methods, capabilities, and vulnerabilities. We committed to memory information on organization, structure, leadership, command and control, weapons, order of battle, strategy and tactics, both political and military. And, over the years between youth and middle age, I'd had the chance to see communism and its effects firsthand in Eastern Europe, Asia, Africa, the Middle East, Cuba, and Central America.

When I went to work at the White House in 1981, there were twenty-two nations around the globe living under the pale of communism. Ronald Reagan, the president I worked for, rightly, I believe, called it an "Evil Empire" and vowed to bring it down. The now-defunct Soviet Union was still the major underwriter for most of these regimes. Massive statues of Russian revolutionary leader Vladimir Ilyich Lenin, standing erect and pointing in patriarchal pose, were prominently placed in the public avenues of capitals from Bucharest to Beijing and from Havana to Hanoi.

But by the time I arrived in Hanoi in 1993, "scientific socialism" had imploded and only five countries remained where Lenin still stood. In Eastern Europe the towering bronzes had all been toppled. Like so many monumental figures before him, Lenin, the great master of Marxism, had gone the way of poet Percy Bysshe Shelley's emblematic Ozymandias of Egypt:

> *"My name is Ozymandias, king of kings,*
> *Look upon my works, ye Mighty, and despair!"*
> *Nothing beside remains. Round the decay*
> *Of that colossal wreck, boundless and bare*
> *The lone and level sands stretch far away.*

But in Hanoi, Lenin's visage has not yet gone the way of Ozymandias. In front of the mausoleum of

Vietnam's own revolutionary hero, Ho Chi Minh, a larger-than-life Lenin still stands erect in a Hanoi park. The scene is ironic. An aging soldier, probably in his mid-sixties, stands comfortably and inconspicuously at his post near Lenin while young children play, oblivious to the presence of either the founding father's towering image or his unarmed, diminutive, and withered attendant. Just a short walk away, inside the monumental, dark gray stone tomb that is guarded by four young troops, Chairman Ho's body is on display in a refrigerated glass case. The founder of Vietnam's Communist Party had asked to be cremated and his ashes scattered, but he was preserved intact by his successors to be venerated by the people. After all, that's what the Russians had done with Lenin's body.

I asked the old soldier, a veteran of wars against the French, the Americans, and his own people to the South, how long he thought the statue of Lenin would remain standing in this Hanoi park. Based on what has happened to communism since the dissolution of the Soviet Union and from all that I could tell about Vietnam's experiment with a "managed market economy," I had come to at least one solid conclusion: In the middle of the night Ol' Vladimir Ilyich should be gently removed from his pedestal, carefully wrapped and boxed up, and put away for safe-keeping. Like a rare, old coin, this statue is a collector's item and would probably be worth something someday.

Had I suggested such a plan to a few of the younger people we met while we were in Hanoi, I would not have been surprised to hear that a heist had taken place in the middle of the night. Outside of government, the new generation of Vietnamese growing up in Hanoi seems to have little concern for the institutions of communism and far greater interest in moving their country forward as part of the international community and an active participant in a global marketplace.

The Communist party officials we met have a somewhat different, though not altogether opposite, agenda. The party functionaries clearly have a greater stake in maintaining the status quo. Their careers, social status, and general well-being are tied to perpetuating institutions that were established to fulfill Lenin's vision and make venerable "Uncle Ho's" dream a reality. But even among these "up-and-coming" apparatchiks, there appear to be few illusions concerning communism. It became clear to all of us on the trip that the bright young party officials we met both admire America and look with anticipation toward the day when they can assume leading roles in transforming Vietnam into something better than it is now. Generally careful not to be openly rebellious or "counter-revolutionary," they gave us the clear impression that they are not taken by the "party line." They were impressively straightforward and businesslike and generally avoided the polemic diatribes about "imperialism" and "capitalist oppressors" so common to discussions with Communist officials.

The only exceptions to this polite, forthright approach we found were in the organs and ministries whose role it is to perpetuate the myths of communism or to memorialize a particular version of history. For those future visitors to Hanoi who may wish to take this "guilt trip," for that's indeed what it is, the best place to start is the People's Army Museum. Unlike the war veterans I met, some of whom I had fought directly against, the people who guide you on these tours have not forgotten, will not forgive, and will have you remember, please, that as an American you are indeed an "oppressive, capitalist war-mongering, supporter of tyrannical puppet regimes." It was oh, so reminiscent of the 1960s and early '70s that I had a definite sense of *déjà vu*.

In fact, the scripted remarks of our museum guides were so clearly the sort of political propaganda that we heard from the anti-war organizations during The War that I concluded much of it had to have come from Hanoi's American friends of that era. As if to substantiate that judgment, many of the photos on the museum's walls were of Hollywood luminaries and American political figures who had, in the words of our guide, "established solidarity with the socialist vanguard" in Hanoi two decades before.

It was also clear to me that this display, somewhat akin to what one would expect of the indoctrination in a reeducation camp, is nothing new. One of the really informative aspects of the war museum is the diorama, film and slide exhibit of the Dien Bien Phu battlefield of 1954. According to our guide, this display had been assembled in the late 1960s to show to foreign visitors. Today it is a regular feature for school children visiting their nation's capital. Notwithstanding the political rhetoric interspersed in the English translation (and, I'm confident, every other language as well) it was, from the perspective of a military man, very impressive. It was all the more so for me in that I have now met several veterans, French and Vietnamese, who fought on both sides of that battle.

As we neared the end of our tour at the museum, our guide asked me if I had any questions. She had just pointed out a display of expended U.S. ordnance, aircraft fuel pods, and air-dropped seismic devices and described them as "American chemical, biological, and nuclear weapons," supposedly used in Vietnam. "Do you really believe all this?" I inquired.

Her reply was a fascinating, if inadvertent, confession: "That is not important. This is what I have been told to say."

It is no secret that while Hanoi won the war and reunified Vietnam under one flag, the people of the South and their way of life have not been fully transformed into the socialist ideal. Although it was renamed Ho Chi Minh City, to this day Saigon remains Saigon. While the conduct of day-to-day commerce certainly changed there in 1975, any contemporary visitor to the two major cities could not miss the contrast. Hanoi is a political capital emerging from the reign of communism. In the wake of abandonment by Moscow, its leaders are trying to learn the ways of global commerce and have conceded that a market economy is essential for the improvement of conditions in this poorest of Asian countries. The most ideologically entrenched remnants of the Communist old guard are found in Hanoi, and the people there have little knowledge of or experience with capitalism let alone democracy.

Saigon, on the other hand, is the country's commercial capital. And Hanoi relies heavily upon the old South Vietnam capital for the country's much needed income. While there are productive rice fields not far from Hanoi itself, most of the country's largest export and dietary staple is grown in the Mekong Delta and is shipped from Saigon.

As though communism's role there is little more than a nuisance, Saigon's bustling marketplace gives the appearance of a world dramatically different from Hanoi. Though I never got to Saigon during The War, some of those who did, and who have since been back, say that today it looks little different from the city they remember in the 1960s and early '70s. Busy shops line the streets, selling everything from televisions to motorcycles, from shoes to pots and pans. It alone among Vietnam's cities is commercially ready to explode, and when it does, the whole region will surely be shaken.

The government in Hanoi, not unaware of the attractiveness of Saigon, is making every effort to lure investors from around the globe further north in Vietnam. While not turning away those who would set up in what they call Ho Chi Minh City, the government's enticements focus on the North, especially the Hanoi area. A possible significant step toward making the country's capital more attractive to businessmen comes in the form of simple, Western creature comfort. While we were there in 1993, much was made of a new thirty-three-million dollar, Singapore-funded, five-star hotel that is scheduled to be built by the end of 1994. Yet, there may be some visitors to Hanoi who will still find these new accommodations less than desirable. The site it will occupy is presently the location of an older, far less comfortable abode: the infamous Hanoi Hilton.

We went to the old POW prison while we were in Hanoi and found that it is still being used today for its original purpose, though those who are held inside, we were assured, are all "petty thieves and common criminals." It was eerie to walk beside the high, concrete wall with its five strands of electrified barbed wire on top and its peeling yellow paint and to recall that it was once the site of so much sadness and brutality for so many Americans. Somehow, our tour guides had neglected to include the old POW compound on our itinerary until we asked.

It is no secret that at the end of the war the South was pillaged. The plunder included everything that had become an ordinary part of life in South Vietnam but was rare or unavailable in the North. At one medical facility in the South that I visited in 1993, a senior staff member was frank when asked about the hospital's lack of equipment. "In 1975," the doctor told me, "the Communists removed all our X-ray machines, incubators, and other equipment, too." He supposed it had been sent to Hanoi. If it had been, we certainly didn't see any evidence of it when we were there. But if his supposition was correct, since all of it was Western-made, repair parts would have become nearly impossible to get. And while some could be cannibalized for a time, eventually this war booty would have become useless junk littering the rooms and corridors of institutions where they had been reinstalled.

For a decade and a half after the war, Communist Vietnam's primary sources of technology were

Warsaw Pact nations. Before its dissolution, the Soviet Union and its allies offered significant loans, technical assistance, and help in building roads, bridges, and buildings. The patrimony of Russian aid has proved not to be a particularly rich or enduring one, however. As we drove about Vietnam in 1993, I noticed numerous Soviet-style buildings that had been abandoned in the middle of construction. Apparently the money for their completion simply ran out.

During a recent visit with Bill Kimball, president of Vets with a Mission, who has gone back to Vietnam repeatedly over the last six years, he affirmed an observation that we had made during our April '93 trip: "Isn't it amazing how almost nothing the Russians put there still works. The revetments that we built at the airfield in Da Nang almost thirty years ago are still there. The port and handling equipment we installed there and in Saigon twenty-five years ago are still in operation. But stuff the Russians built or delivered just four and five years ago is already falling apart."

He might have been thinking of the Dong Ha hotel where we stayed for two nights during our 1993 visit. The telltale, institutional, cinderblock architecture allowed no mistaking the fact: Russians had built it—and less than a decade earlier. While the smiling faces of the hotel employees betrayed their industriousness and eagerness to serve and the pleasure and pride they took in their work, the facility itself was a wreck. From the cracked cement and crumbling mortar outside to its peeling and faded paint and sagging windows, the structure was a shambles. Thanks to the diligence of those on duty, it was possible to get same-day laundry service. But the shower in my room was nothing more than a four-foot length of garden hose. Clearly, it had once been jammed into a hand-held spray nozzle that could still be found in the bathroom, but there is no telling how long it had just been sitting there.

David Roth and I were roommates on the trip. As we were settling down for our first night in Dong Ha, the two of us opened the mosquito nets that were stowed away in the wall over our beds. They were the fold-out kind with extendable arms from which the mesh is draped. I should have known immediately that there was something wrong when the suspended netting began closing in on me. By morning I was wrapped, cocoon-like, in mosquito netting. Upon close inspection of the two nets, David and I noticed there was an important difference between his frame and mine. Though both had the identical Cyrillic markings, mine had been made without a crossbar to hold the arms apart.

Had we not been so tired, the giant Russian-built air conditioner on the wall might have kept us awake. With its mighty sound the unit could have been expected to produce a great, continual blast of cold air, like a fierce, driving, Siberian wind. Yet, for all the noise, our room was little cooler than the tropics outside. Worse yet, this supposed air conditioner produced an odor similar to that generated by a diesel truck. We consoled ourselves with the thought that at least we had not released any freon into the atmosphere and further enlarged the hole in the ozone layer.

Our hotel was just one of many examples of the chronically dilapidated condition of things left behind by the Russians. But perhaps the most interesting exemplar of a lasting legacy in Vietnam is in the language. Nearly everyone we met could speak at least some English. Nobody I asked could speak any Russian.

If Russian communism left the people of what once had been South Vietnam with unfulfilled expectations, their unrestrained joy at seeing Americans twenty years after our having abandoned them may well be indicative of fond memories from the past, their resilient, forgiving nature, and their hope for the future. The generation of younger adults in their twenties and thirties, including most of our "keepers" who kept a watch on us and got us to where we were going, very likely spent their earliest years suffering from the effects of the American withdrawal and the war's final years. But few of them appeared easily deceived by the Party's old-fashioned propaganda filled with anti-imperialist slogans.

That does not keep them from becoming what by all accounts would be considered good party members, and for good reason. Status and privilege, along with substantial mobility and significant financial benefits, are among the perks of ascending the ranks within the Party and the government. In many ways, however, their motivations and benefits are precisely those of market capitalism.

In the South I was surprised to hear local People's Committee members being openly critical of the national government and even publicly stepping out of line concerning communism itself. A senior government official who said he had fought as a Viet Cong soldier, literally spat on the ground as if at the Party Central Committee when the subject of the Hanoi government was raised. Another local official quietly tipped us to the presence of a member of the secret police who had been following us. We thanked him, though we weren't particularly surprised. In Da Nang we had noticed that we were being surreptitiously videotaped as one of our own cameras was rolling for the documentary we were shooting. We turned our camera on their clandestine cameraman who was recording us with a long lens from a spot across the street and down the block from our hotel. For a few comic moments the two cameras were shooting each other when suddenly the Vietnamese cameraman realized what was happening. He abruptly shut his camera off, jumped onto the back of a motorcycle, and was speedily driven away. We saw him again, days later, in Ho Chi Minh City. By then we had nicknamed him the "Candid Cameraman," and his superiors must have decided to stop playing games and "go overt." As our crew filmed outside the former American Embassy, he recorded my potentially provocative remarks while standing right next to our cameramen who had caught him on tape only days before.

Unlike the "Candid Cameraman" who would never speak with us, we did have the opportunity to get to know the young men who traveled with us. Though some were members of the Ministry of Health, our hosts for the trip, and another was with the Foreign Ministry, several were from the Interior Ministry. In Communist countries these folks don't run the national parks. The Interior Ministry is in charge of things like good order and discipline and ensuring that the "party line" is carefully followed. Yet these young men were all friendly, courteous, and helpful. On our final day one asked us to mail a letter to a family member in the United States. Another wanted us to send him an English-language book about the war. We asked several of our "keepers" what they thought about the U.S.A. Each time there was no suppressing the gleam in their eyes. One said, "It's a great nation, a wonderful nation, yes, a very great nation."

And they had observed, more than once, other Vietnamese we met in our travels as they asked us to "take me with you," anticipating our return to American soil. But not the bright, young party men. They are savvy and calculating. They just seem to be waiting for America's return to Vietnam—and for the opportunity to get in at the ground level.

21

HOSPITALS

Vietnam: 1968, 1993

WHILE MUCH ABOUT VIETNAM HAD CHANGED SINCE I
was first there in 1968, there were several places we
visited in 1993 where I found many parallels to my
experience twenty-five years before—the hospitals.
That's not to say that they're the same now as they
were then or that the standard of treatment is even
remotely the same. But the hospitals were then and
are now places where desperately injured or ill people receive loving treatment from physicians and
nurses who care deeply and struggle desperately to
save their patients. But that's where the similarity
ends.

During The War, the U.S. military established a
string of sophisticated medical facilities that covered
the length of South Vietnam. As a rule, a wounded

soldier, sailor, airman, or Marine, could be receiving major medical treatment in fewer than thirty minutes from the time he was injured or wounded. And these modern, well-equipped and expertly staffed facilities were backed up by U.S. naval hospital ships offshore and, where necessary, rapid air evacuation in specially configured USAF "Nightingale" medevac aircraft that could jet a patient to Japan or even the United States for more advanced treatment.

On three different occasions I wound up in the 3d Medical Battalion hospital in Quang Tri. The first time, in February 1969, I was badly hurt when the revolving turret of the tank I was riding on batted me like a baseball in the midst of a firefight along the DMZ. I arrived in Quang Tri on a helicopter with several other Marines from my platoon who were wounded in the same engagement. Unfortunately, our arrival coincided with several other flights of wounded from other units. The triage was full of casualties on litters, some stretched across saw horses, others simply placed on the floor.

The purpose of triage is to rapidly sort and prioritize casualties so that those who need the most immediate medical treatment receive it fastest. But when a facility is overwhelmed, as 3d Med was on that bleak day in February 1969, the doctors and corpsmen would often have the worst task of all: selecting from the crowd of broken men those who were likely to survive and placing them in sequence for surgery. Because of the physical limits of the facilities and the number of doctors, they would have to leave until last those who, from the nature of their trauma, appeared least likely to live.

On days like these, the surgical suites were packed with doctors and nurses frantically trying to save men with frightfully maimed, burned, and blasted bodies. Out in the triage, corpsmen would add morphine and pain killers to the IV bottles of those who would not make it into surgery, while chaplains would pass among the litters consoling, comforting, and giving the last rites to those who would likely not leave that room alive.

The litter bearers who removed me and my wounded men from the CH-46 medevac helicopter slipped on the blood that covered the deck where we had lain on the flight from the edge of the DMZ. The dead body of Les Shafer, one of my valiant squad leaders, had been loaded aboard with us. I had flown on the floor of that vibrating "bird," propped against the inside wall of the fuselage, with his head cradled on my lap, hoping that somehow he would be revived but knowing better at the same time. As the stretcher bearers gently placed us on litters, I watched as the aviation crew chief hosed our blood off the helicopter's ramp. They then rushed us off the hot tarmac into the shade of the tin-roofed triage shed with the large, red cross painted on its sunbaked surface.

The green canvas stretcher I was on was placed across two sawhorses. Things happen fast in triage. Almost immediately, a Navy medical corpsman was alongside starting an IV, while another used some kind of electric cutter to slice through my mud- and blood-caked clothing, webbed pistol belt, and flak jacket. I watched as my now useless camouflage shirt, trousers, gear, and boots, all neatly shorn in pieces, were thrown into a large plastic bag along with my pistol, grenades, ammunition, and gas mask. As one of them marked the bag with information copied from my dog tags, I remember wanting to tell them to take the pistol out of the holster so that it wouldn't rust. I didn't have the energy or breath to say the words. Then, as one of the corpsmen was starting to pump up the cuff to measure my blood pressure, I looked up to see Chaplain Jake Laboon, our regimental chaplain.

Jake was a legend and a close friend. He had graduated from the Naval Academy in World War II and was decorated for bravery as a submarine officer in the war against Japan. After the war he became a Jesuit priest and returned to the Navy as a chaplain. I had come to know him well at Annapolis, where he had served when I was a midshipman. Now we were together again in the 3d Marines. He looked at the blood bubbling out of my nose and mouth from a collapsed left lung. He patted my shoulder. At the approach of the medical officer who had the ghastly task of sorting those who would at least have a chance to live from those who probably would not, he leaned down to me and said, "Perk up." And then to the Doc he said something like, "Probably ought to take my friend here—he looks pretty good."

The trip to surgery was quick. A vacuum tube inserted into the chest cavity reinflated my lung, pain killers numbed the discomfort, antibiotics prevented infection, and I made the kind of rapid recovery so common to healthy young men in the prime of their lives.

That was the kind of treatment that a U.S. casualty received almost anywhere in Vietnam twenty-five years ago. For the wounded South Vietnamese soldier it was very nearly the same. Medevac helicopters, modern technology and equipment, well-trained physicians, all courtesy of the United States, were all available as long as we were there, fighting alongside them.

Twenty-five years later it seemed that the entire country had taken a giant medical leap backward. Gone were the modern, highly efficient hospitals and clinics that had saved so many lives. In their place are the remnants of a tragically inadequate medical system incapable of providing anything close to what is needed by a population of nearly seventy million people. A sad parallel between then and now is that some of the most shocking and tragic scenes in the whole country can still be found in Vietnam's hospitals.

The poor conditions of the facilities themselves are only exceeded by the limitations on patient care. But it is not for a lack of doctors. In fact, the doctor-to-patient ratio in Vietnam's hospitals may be among the best in the world. In one hospital with 300 beds there were 100 doctors. Another had only 100 beds but 93 physicians. Vietnam does not need more doctors. It is everything else that is needed.

The field hospital in Quang Tri where my men and I had received lifesaving treatment is, of course, long gone. In fact, since the invasion in 1972, so is most of Quang Tri city. Today, in its place is the Quang Tri Provincial Hospital in Dong Ha. This is the only major medical facility in the entire province, and we went to see it in April '93. I was stunned by a sight that would be simply unheard of even in the poorest and most antiquated of American medical facilities. In an open-air corridor stood a rack of used rubber surgical gloves, washed and hanging up to dry. Gloves, we were told, are hard to come by and very expensive. Therefore they are used and re-used until they are torn or so brittle that they crack.

But it wasn't only gloves. Syringes are used over and over again, too. Naturally, doctors are concerned about the possibility of transmitting disease through used needles, but they insist that every effort is being made to ensure that both gloves and syringes are as sterile as possible, even though their sterilization equipment is unbelievably primitive. In facilities where surgery is often performed without electric lights, where operating rooms are frequently cooled by the occasional light tropical breeze blowing through open windows as flies circle, all taken-for-granted Western standards of hygiene are an elusive and distant ideal. It is not that they don't know any better. The sad fact is that they can't *do* any better.

It is therefore no surprise that every delivery of supplies and equipment made by relief organizations such as International Aid is eagerly awaited, sincerely appreciated, and put to very good immediate use by the Vietnamese. Accompanied by IA's president and CEO, Ralph Plumb, and Dr. Jack Henderson, its medical director, I saw scenes the likes of which I had never before witnessed. As I toured the hospital, the laboratory could have been a museum exhibit at the Smithsonian, though the equipment was probably too dilapidated to be up to the Smithsonian's standard. It might however have fit in a 1930s Frankenstein movie.

Each corridor was a further step into medical horror: patients quite often two or more to a bed; major pieces of equipment such as X-ray machines, all of it decades out-of-date, collecting dust, and rusting for lack of repair parts.

With the exception of medical facilities in what was once Yugoslavia, the Quang Tri Province hospital may have the highest number of patients suffering from the effects of exploding ordnance of any hospital in the world today. But the ordnance that is killing and maiming the children of Quang Tri isn't being fired from guns today, it is from "left-over" bombs, mines, and shells on old battlefields. Hospital officials claim that in 1992, 720 operations were conducted as a result of such tragedies. There were twelve deaths. But of those who survived, nearly every patient was seriously maimed for life.

Dr. B. V. Tinh, of Quang Tri's provincial hospital, showed us around his facility. On our brief tour we saw two young girls in adjacent beds who were injured in the same accident and admitted a week earlier. The younger girl was perhaps twelve years old, the same age as my youngest daughter. She lost her left foot and the lower half of her calf from what was described to us as an artillery shell found in a rice field. Her teenage friend took a piece of shrapnel under the arm, severing the radial nerve and rendering her left arm limp. And there were others. A young man, perhaps in his twenties, had his pelvis broken and suffered abdominal injuries. On his right hand two fingers were missing and the other three were mangled. An innocent six-year-old boy, Nguyen Li, was rolling back and forth on his cot, forlorn. He had lost a hand and an eye only days before. These victims of the war that has yet to end were pleading for our help, but there was nothing we could do to restore their lost members. And as our eyes met, I could see once again the old look of terror, or desperate sadness, the look I knew from a quarter century before—the heart-breaking look of war.

Interestingly enough, none of the dozens of medical personnel we met in Vietnam made a single reference to the source of the munitions that had caused these devastating injuries. They didn't care if the mortar round or mine or grenade that maimed their little patients had been made in Vietnam, the People's Republic of China, the U.S.A., or the USSR. All they cared about was how to they could treat the injuries. The only person who made any comment at all about this issue was an American. She was associated with another aid organization that had been involved in Vietnam since the 1960s. It was clear that her agenda was different from ours.

"Don't you feel just terrible, seeing all the casualties that unexploded American munitions have caused?" she asked.

"You know, you are the only person to have raised that since I've been here," I replied. "It might interest you to know that when we were at Con Thien the other day, a little girl handed me a Soviet antipersonnel mine with the fuse still in it. I don't think either one of us would have cared too much about where it was made if it had gone off at that moment. The war is over, let it be. We're here trying to help people because as Christians we believe that's what we're supposed to do." Somehow I doubt that the message got through.

As severe and numerous as they are, injuries from ordnance are the second most common reason for hospital admissions in Quang Tri Province. By far the largest number of patients there and throughout Vietnam's hospitals are being treated for malaria. The Quang Tri provincial hospital admitted more than 1500 malaria patients in 1992. Fortunately, all but eight recovered. But the real death toll from malaria is probably much higher, for many who are ill never get to the hospital and die at home.

The part of the world that twenty-five years ago had the fastest medical evacuation in the world, today has no ambulances except in major cities. Someone who is sick or injured near the Laotian border or on what was once the Khe Sanh battlefield can easily spend more than a day getting to the hospital in Dong Ha. Many choose not to even try to make the journey. Others never survive it.

After malaria and ordnance-related injuries, malnutrition is the next most likely cause for admission to a hospital. The fourfold plague of the Third World: starvation, dehydration, malnutrition, and dysentery—no food, no water, bad food, bad water—is not at its worst in Vietnam. There is food and water, but for many the meager diet is nutritionally imbalanced, and their water is tainted by bacterial diseases.

One area where the assistance of International Aid has been particularly beneficial is in the treatment of hydrocephalic children, those with "water on the brain," whose distinctive characteristic is an enlarged head. Untreated, or treated too late, the condition causes serious brain damage, or even death. In the West, medical technology has rendered hydrocephalus a condition that is fairly easy to treat and almost never life-threatening. A simple shunt is implanted at the base of the skull, and a small tube, or catheter, implanted under the skin extends to the abdomen. Excess fluid flows through the tube and is disposed of as human waste.

It was heartbreaking to see Vietnamese children in need of such a simple procedure, some of whom were beyond the point of treatment or whose brain damage was already severe. But unlike the United States where we tend to take for granted the availability of most medical procedures, the Vietnamese have come to expect that while medical procedures are free, they are often also unavailable. Though the technology and procedure for hydrocephalus are commonly available in the United States, the shunts themselves have been almost impossible to obtain in Vietnam, in large part because of their cost. Resourceful Vietnamese doctors have improvised, creating makeshift drains by using a length of tubing alone; however, these often fail. And in Vietnam even the tubing is almost impossible to come by. On our 1993 trip, International Aid was able to deliver shunts and tubing, donated by Dow Chemical (yes, I recognized the irony—Dow was a favorite target of Vietnam war protestors for manufacturing war materials). Dr. Jack Henderson instructed the physicians on the relatively simple procedure for implanting the device, and we promised to obtain and deliver more.

Wherever we visited a hospital, in the North, the South, and in Central Vietnam, we were reminded of their very basic needs. While it would be nice to have the latest technology, their doctors insisted that expensive machines are only valuable when they come with training for their operators, repair parts, and regular, required service. Of course the people of Vietnam could benefit from the latest MRI, but even more helpful would be a trusty, sturdy X-ray machine and sufficient maintenance and spare parts to keep it operating. At our request, every hospital's administration prepared a "wish list" that could only be seen for what it was—a *needs* list.

One of the major problems facing medical professionals in Vietnam is a very simple but potentially deadly one—secondary infections picked up in the hospital. As we chatted with doctors while walking through corridors, they often asked us to provide them disinfectants and simple sanitary supplies.

Dressed in his white lab coat and hat, a proud, caring Dr. Tinh stood and talked with me about his hospital and its many needs. It was impossible not to notice his sincere concern for so many in such great pain. I inquired about the problem of the sick and injured getting from outlying areas to Dong Ha for treatment. He confirmed that there was a small clinic in Khe Sanh, for example, but they could do no surgery or any major medical procedures there. And there is no ambulance to bring patients across the mostly dirt track called Highway 9 that runs east-west through the province to Dong Ha.

When I was injured in 1969, the medevac helicopter that brought me and my wounded Marines to the hospital at Quang Tri took little more than fifteen minutes to cover the distance from our battlefield on the DMZ to the finest medical treatment in the world. Afterward, I spent several days recuperating at our battalion's aid station in Dong Ha, not far from where his tragically inadequate hospital is located.

When I mentioned this to Dr. Tinh, I did not know that the doctor, too, was a veteran. He recalled for me his own experience of trying to care for NVA wounded. Then he added, "During the war it took fifteen minutes to get medical help, but in peacetime now, it will take fifteen hours to bring people from remote places to our hospital."

He asked if he could add an ambulance to his "wish list."

Then he offered one final appeal: "Under these very difficult conditions we have been able to save many patients. If you can help us more in the future, we will be able to save even more."

"We hope to do just that," I assured him, not knowing exactly how I would fulfill that hope.

22

ENTERPRISE

Vietnam: 1993

WE WERE RETURNING FROM THE LONG TRIP WEST ON Highway 9 when we decided to stop for some gas and a soda. No, we did not pull into the nearest Exxon station. We chose instead the local gas station/restaurant/tailor shop.

It wasn't much to look at. A teenage girl sat beneath her thatched lean-to, hunched over the polished black and silver of her foot-powered, treadle sewing machine, the kind my grandmother had when I was a little boy. And like my grandmother, this young woman was intently focused on keeping the hem straight on whatever she was sewing. On a carefully hand-crafted table beside her was a line-up of beverages, mostly the locally bottled fruit-juice-based punch, but canned Coke as well. So much for

215

the trade embargo. On the shelf below the canned and bottled drinks was a selection of local delicacies; fresh fruit, a dried fish, rice balls, and several other edibles I did not recognize. Between her seat in the shade and the sun-soaked road was the gas station: a five-gallon can with a one-liter plastic bottle next to it, used for measuring the amount of fuel purchased and pouring it into a customer's gas tank.

Our driver got out and ordered a liter of gas. The young restauranteur – seamstress – gas-station attendant smiled and set her sewing aside. She then commenced filling the one-liter bottle from the five-gallon can, using a small funnel to prevent the loss of a single drop of the precious liquid.

"All the way. All the way to the top," our driver insisted. She gave him our money's worth.

We bought refreshments, paid for the food and fuel, piled back into the van, and were on our way. It was faster than stopping at a Seven Eleven on an American interstate.

I had never before been to a gas station where I could have a suit made. But due to our tight schedule, I failed to take advantage of what I correctly suspected was a singular opportunity. I did notice, however, that the service at this establishment was excellent given the station's limitations.

I am not sure how much of her business is tailor-shop, restaurant, or gas station, but it occurred to me that the girl was wasting no time between customers in her varied ventures.

My bet is that this young girl's parents are also enterprising people. Vietnam's new experiment with a market economy has resulted in nearly everyone we met being engaged in some sort of business venture. It seemed as though every structure of any kind that isn't a government office or a military post has some kind of business going on under its roof. Whether it was a home, or just four poles with a tarpaulin or piece of plastic draped over them, somebody seemed to be there making something, selling something, repairing something, or all of the above.

In Saigon we drove down streets where every door was a storefront. A motorcycle-repair shop followed by a new- and used-fender salesman, then a tire place followed by a scrap-metal dealer. Or a pots and pans vendor beside one offering charcoal around the corner from a shop selling ducks, hens, and a variety of exotic edible birds, next to a place where the rice was piled high and pickled eels and snakes were for sale. My favorite was a portable-radio dealer next door to the man who sells only batteries. They had clearly worked out their own "free enterprise" arrangement. The portable radio dealer offered no batteries, and the battery store had no radios to sell, yet, the name on the products in both establishments was the same: Panasonic.

Saigon is still the hub of commercial activity, but in a country where the per-capita income is only around $200 per year you have to wonder how much buying and selling goes on in some of the more remote areas with mere subsistence economies. But even in the relatively isolated parts of the central highlands it was quite common to see a little boy and his sister squatting beside the side of the road with as little as two or three canned soft drinks, hoping that someone passing by on a bicycle would pay a few Vietnamese dong (or even better, U.S. dollars) for a moment's refreshment.

I wanted to see the effects of this experiment in free enterprise in Hanoi, so part of our group went for a walk through an open-air market. I was struck by how the array of stalls and storefronts resembled those in dozens of other places I had visited around the world. There were no luxury items, only staples: food, clothing, building materials, cooking oil, fuel, auto parts, bicycle shops, motorcycle dealers, tire stores, furniture, fabrics, an apothecary, eyeglasses (lenses already ground and installed), pots and pans, plumbing pipe, cooking utensils, and on and on.

The majority of things for sale were similar to those that could be found nearly anywhere—except for the Russian watches, which were proudly displayed as novelty items, apparently for Japanese and Western tourists like us. One of our cameramen, Jack Pagano, who had himself been to the Soviet Union just before the collapse of communism, stocked up on Russian watches—not because they ran so well but as souvenirs for his friends at home who had admired the one he'd obtained where it originated. Jack wanted nothing to do with the latest version of the Russian watches bearing images of Boris Yeltsin and the Russian tri-color flag. He bought only the ones with a red hammer and sickle. Going price: $15. Like the system that had produced them, none of them worked.

Betsy and I often go looking in the stores at a local mall at home in Virginia, but I rarely buy anything. I never have been much of a shopper. True to form, in Hanoi I mostly looked. But I wanted to make a purchase in this market for two reasons. First, I simply wanted to have the experience of conducting business—picking out something that interested me, inquiring about its price, striking a deal, paying for it, and walking away with a purchase. Second, I was so impressed with what free enterprise seemed to be doing for the material and social well-being of the people of Vietnam that I wanted to make at least some token contribution to capitalism's conquest.

Besides, every man—socialist or capitalist—can use a tie. So I looked for a stall that had some fairly attractive ones.

The place where I stopped was a combination tie-and-jewelry store with a small sideline of Zippo lighters, ballpoint pens, herbal medicines, and spices. They may have sold sandals and Marlboro cigarettes in there as well, but on second thought, those two items may have belonged to the auto-parts store next door on the sidewalk. It occurred to me to ask what kind of retail licenses were required in this new "managed market," but I didn't want to give our government guides any fresh ideas about how we in the West have tried to stifle entrepreneurship and enterprise.

I picked out a nice conservative red-white-and-blue silk tie that looked like it was made just for me. "The price?" I asked.

"Three dollars," the woman behind the watch case said in English.

"Sold!" I replied.

She put the tie in a paper bag for me as I got out three one dollar bills. We made our exchange. "Thank you sir," she added. I smiled back at her and returned the thank-you. We both seemed convinced that we'd gotten a good deal.

A number of years ago there was a drought in Vietnam that devastated the rice fields. They were, at that time, owned and managed by communism's great euphemism for governmental bureaucracy—"the people." This natural disaster created a critical shortage of the nation's most essential dietary staple. Shortly thereafter the government began allowing families once again to farm their own plots of land. Although there are no exact figures available, not surprisingly, the productivity of those fields was multiplied when they reverted to a system where individual initiative is rewarded. My guess is that it won't be long before the market economy transforms Vietnamese society. No one, not even the most entrenched and hardened Communist, wants to sit back and watch the opportunities, brought on by the obvious demise of the Marxist-Leninist experiment, pass by.

23

THE CHILDREN OF WAR

Vietnam: 1969, 1993

MOST AMERICANS KNOW LITTLE OF ORPHANS AND orphanages. In a society where the possibility of children is often precluded by contraception, and unwanted pregnancies are aborted, what was only two generations ago a venerable institution—the orphanage—has virtually disappeared.

Not so in Vietnam.

From the north to the south, orphanages dot the landscape. Most are in cities, but they are found everywhere, these homes for children whose parents have either died or are unable to care for them.

The orphanage I saw outside Da Nang, not far from where I once fought, had been a ministry of the Catholic church that still stands next door but for nearly twenty years has been closed. When the

221

Communists took over and closed the churches, this orphanage was kept open. Its present director, Ho Vietine, had been there before 1975 and was allowed to continue caring for children there.

He was a particularly gracious older man, dressed up in what was most certainly his only jacket and tie. We were honored by the hospitality he offered our sometimes hard-to-manage entourage of fifteen. From the moment I began talking with him it was clear to see that he loved the eighty children under his care. Perhaps a quarter of them became orphaned not by the death of their parents but because of their severe birth defects and their parents' inability to care for them. Some of these children are unable to move from their beds; others could get around but were disfigured. Others were "economic orphans"—their parents simply did not have the means to provide for them. Whatever the circumstances that brought these children there, all of them were cared for.

Most of the children were healthy. They possessed little more than the clothing they wore on their backs, but like the orphanage's buildings, every one of them was clean and each child we saw wore a priceless smile.

I was deeply impressed and moved. This little man had given his life for these homeless children. He had little to work with but his love for them. And despite the pain suffered by some of the little ones, each one knew the love of this special man.

As I toured his facility, I noticed through a window that J. C. Huizinga, one of our traveling companions, was in the courtyard, surrounded by children. Through the most oppressively hot and humid days in Vietnam, J. C. always seemed to be having a good time. And the kids especially loved him. They called him the "smiling Buddha," and I'll let you guess why.

On this particular stop he was busy taking Polaroid photos of the children in twos and threes, then giving them the photos. Instead of buying souvenirs on our trip, he gave them away. Watching the faces of the children as their photographic images slowly appeared before their eyes would alone have been worth making the trip. J. C. shot ten packages of instant film, and when he ran out he gave away the camera, too, promising to bring more film with him on his next trip. We proudly dubbed him our Ambassador of Polaroid.

Among the most sorrowful orphans we saw on our 1993 visit to Vietnam aren't even Vietnamese—at least they are not regarded as such by the people of Vietnam. These lonely children are the offspring of Vietnamese mothers and American fathers—in most cases, soldiers, sailors, airmen, and Marines who served in Vietnam from the early 1960s through the early 1970s.

Except for tourists and foreign businessmen, everyone we saw on the streets of Hanoi looked Vietnamese. Of course, during The War there had been no Americans in the North. But as soon as we traveled south of the DMZ, and especially on our brief trip through Ho Chi Minh City, every so often we would glimpse someone who looked racially different. Some were fairer, others were noticeably more dark, nearly all were taller than the average Vietnamese. They are the children of war and are called "Amerasians."

Americans have become accustomed to interracial marriages and interracial children. But unlike America, the ethnic and racial "melting pot" is atypical of much of the rest of the world. Most traditional societies still cherish racial, ethnic, or tribal "purity." There are specific cultural rules proscribing who may marry whom. Despite Marxism's egalitarian rhetoric, among the Vietnamese who are traditionally proud of their cultural and ethnic distinctiveness, Amerasians are commonly treated as a social and racial aberration.

The consequences of prejudice and discrimination are a way of life for these children who, twenty years after the Americans left Southeast Asia, are now adults themselves. Many have children of their own. All are outcasts.

Our visit to the Amerasian Transit Center in Saigon was a melancholy experience. Typically shunned and scorned as they have grown up in their mothers' native land, those who make it to this walled residential center live in a cultural limbo, cut off from the Vietnamese whose homes are just outside. Everyone staying at the transit center has been approved by the American government for relocation in the U.S. and eventually will board a plane that will take them on a life-changing journey across the Pacific.

According to Le Van Thien, the director of the center and a former Viet Cong soldier, more than 70,000 Amerasians and their family members have left Vietnam for the U.S. since the war ended. More than 50,000 of those have been processed through the center since it was established in 1990, and approximately 18,000 leave each year under the provisions of the 1987 Amerasian Homecoming Act.

This legislation allows Amerasians to bring their own spouses and children, as well as parents, with them. The ratio of those who immigrate seems to be about two to one—typically, two family members accompany each Amerasian in this personal exodus. In all, about 30,000 Amerasians have come to the States to date.

There is no way to count how many American servicemen fathered children in Vietnam, and it is almost impossible to get an accurate count of how many Amerasian children there are. Le Van Thien estimates, probably conservatively, that about 35,000 sons and daughters of American troops remain in Vietnam. That is the same number as those who have applied to come to the United States and are in the process of evaluation.

The process, which hinges on demonstrating one's American lineage, is a long one. For those whose physical features are clearly Caucasian or African-American, further proof is not required. For those whose looks are arguably Vietnamese the process is much more difficult. Often it takes five years. In the best of cases the wait is at least a year. Once the way has been cleared with U.S. government officials based in Bangkok, arrangements are made for the Amerasian, along with family members, to be relocated to one of forty-nine regional sites in the United States. One of these is not far from my home, in northern Virginia.

The visit to the Amerasian Transit Center was disquieting. Adult children of American fathers and Vietnamese mothers, now citizens of Vietnam and soon to be bona fide Americans, are gathered into the compound. There are a hundred Amerasians at any particular time, accompanied by about two hundred family members. By Vietnamese standards, the living conditions are quite good.

When my traveling companions and I were given a tour of the facility, we were swarmed by the young men. A tall, blue-eyed twenty-one-year-old with Asian features showed me a small snapshot of his father. I was not sure whether he offered it proudly or was hoping I might be the key to finding the man who gave him life, and whom he never knew. A pair of girls whose father was certainly black, pointed, looked at us out of the side of their almond-shaped eyes, smiled, then turned shyly away. A dark-skinned, short-haired, young man sat on a stoop like a tough guy. His body was heavily tattooed. He looked as though he had come from the "hood"—except for the unmistakably, slight Vietnamese body. An exotically statuesque young woman, maybe twenty-five years old, stood apart. Her mix of Caucasian and Asian features seemed to be the most refined of both her parents. One young black-Vietnamese couple proudly showed us their newborn baby. The baby's grandmother, once the companion of an American GI, looked on with a smile.

Tragically, fewer than 500 Americans who served in Vietnam have made official inquiries about children they left behind. Of course, some fathers returned stateside without ever knowing that the women whose company they kept had borne them children. Others may have left the country intending to keep in touch but didn't. Some made a choice not to "complicate matters at home."

War *is* a taste of hell. And in hell the order and sanity that God created and intended is turned upside down. It all began in the Garden with Adam and Eve and the Fall. What was in essence good, became disordered. The effect of that disorder touches all of us; there is no escaping the fact that men and women are frail, flawed creatures with a sinful, fallen nature.

In war, generally good men are asked to do fundamentally evil things that they would not otherwise do for what are believed to be good purposes in the end. For many who served in The War, the confusion and frustration and hopelessness of the situation often became a license to cast aside personal responsibilities and the consequences of one's actions. Though war may be hell, good men can come through it—those whose lives are not cut short either by physical death or an emotional equivalent—on the side of the angels.

As I have thought about the Amerasians of Vietnam, scorned by Vietnamese society and abandoned by their American fathers, two thoughts come to mind. The first is that the Judeo-Christian tradition asserts that we are all created in the image and likeness of God. God made us all with a fundamental dignity and worth. Christians believe that the saving work of Jesus was for all, and that all are "precious in His sight." The treatment these children of God have received in their native land is reprehensible. Though it took a full decade for the American government to open its borders to these, our own, the "homecoming" is meritorious.

My second observation runs the risk of turning

preachy and may be disturbing to some, but it is less a moralizing note than a simple recognition—every child deserves a father.

Maybe it is because I had a loving father and I am one myself.

24

ON RETREAT

Vietnam: 1993

RELIGIOUS TENSIONS ARE NOT NEW TO VIETNAM. The origins of religious friction pre-date the French colonial era and go all the way back to Chinese attempts to subjugate their Annamite neighbors to the south. In modern times, religious strains are also tied to political passions and changes. After the French defeat in 1954 and the partition of the country at the 17th parallel, tens of thousands of Catholics fled to the new Republic of Vietnam. In the early 1960s the hostility of the Buddhist majority toward the predominantly Catholic Diem regime boiled over into the streets of South Vietnam's major cities.

On May 8, 1963, more than 20,000 Buddhists gathered in Vietnam's ancient capital, the historic city of Hue, to celebrate the Buddha's birthday.

The peaceful march became violent. Seven children, one woman, and a man were killed and another twenty were wounded when an ARVN unit opened fire on the crowd on orders from one of President Diem's local officials. The government tried to blame the Viet Cong.

A month later, the MACV commander, General Paul Harkins, warned American military personnel to avoid duty with ARVN units that were suppressing Buddhists. The world took note when a Buddhist monk, Quang Duc, stepped out of a car and onto a busy Saigon street and immolated himself with gasoline and a match as a public protest of the government's actions and as a plea for "compassion and charity" toward all religions. Diem's sister-in-law referred to the incident, and others like it that followed, as "barbecues" and offered to supply matches to anyone else who was interested.

By the time that I arrived in Vietnam in 1968, the self-immolation of Buddhist monks was a ritual form of protest against the Diem regime. Yet, during my tour of duty, I didn't witness any religious oppression, or even religious tension. In the remote firebases of northern I Corps, we had relatively little contact or interaction with the civilian population, and religion wasn't something we discussed with the Vietnamese we saw the most: the NVA.

After the collapse of the South in 1975, the new rulers began a strict crackdown as part of their effort to "consolidate" the country under Communist rule from Hanoi. The small Christian community was hit hard and hit often. Within a matter of months, virtually all churches were closed. Though the Buddhist population and their pagodas never experienced quite the level of oppression levied against the ten percent Christian population, religion of all sorts was harshly discouraged. Catholic priests and bishops were interred in so-called reeducation camps. The nation's archbishop was exiled to Rome. Other priests who had been studying abroad were denied reentry to their native land. In August 1988 all priests were released from the reeducation camps but still not permitted to resume their pastoral duties.

Despite officially denied efforts to suppress religion, refugees from Vietnam paint quite another picture. And they also tell another, more inspiring story about a small but growing church movement that has not only endured but is quietly flourishing today. Protestant home churches have sprung up throughout Vietnam, especially in the South. Formerly closed churches have been gradually reopening, the government is beginning to allow new churches to be formed to minister to the Vietnamese people. Permission was recently granted, however, to open a new, international, interdenominational church in Ho Chi Minh City to serve the spiritual needs of the ever-growing numbers of foreign businessmen, aid workers, and tourists. It is particularly significant that this church is being founded by a group of Americans called Vets with a Mission.

At the Bangkok hotel where we stayed overnight en route to Hanoi, our group was met by Michael Hoa Viola Vu, the Vietnam Program Director for Bethany Christian Services, and two other Christian activists, one an American and the other an exiled Vietnamese, both of whom work with Christian groups in Vietnam. Because both men travel frequently to Vietnam and are at risk because of the work, we'll call them John and Kim. John was on his way into Vietnam, but Kim had just been turned away at the airport, denied reentry to Vietnam because of his "unsavory counter-revolutionary activities"—in other words, the active practice of Christianity.

Kim, an ordained Pentecostal pastor, had fled Vietnam at the end of the war and eventually became the head of a Vietnamese congregation in the U.S. In recent years he had been involved in relief efforts to Vietnam and returned there thirteen times. While in his native country, however, he also participated in a variety of evangelical activities, especially teaching local groups of Christians. On his most recent arrival in Hanoi he was met at the airport by something less than a welcoming committee. Despite his having an entry visa granted by the Vietnamese government, a decree from the Ministry of the Interior branded him *persona non grata* and he was put back on the plane to return to Bangkok.

The People's Committee of Da Nang had given him approval to enter the country, and he was granted a visa. The Hanoi government turned him back. Back in Bangkok, FAXes were exchanged, and he was again informed by the Da Nang People's Committee that he was welcome and that a new visa had been granted. Within hours, however, he was informed, again by the Interior Ministry in Hanoi, that his second set of travel documents was no longer valid. Kim and John described this on-again-off-again treatment as either a case of the proverbial bureaucratic right hand not knowing what the left is doing, or the tale of a society, government, and set of philosophical tenets in flux. On the other hand, they concluded, it could be a bit of both. In either case, we were told, Kim's story is not an unusual one.

On a walk through the streets of Hanoi, we came upon what clearly had once been a beautiful French neo-gothic Catholic Church on a neighborhood square. But it was gray from years without care. The steps were grimy and littered. Out in front stood a traditional statue of Jesus' mother, Mary. There was no doubt to us that the church building had been closed for years. Yet, someone had put a bouquet of fresh-cut flowers at the foot of the statue.

One of the great surprises of our trip was in Da Nang. We looked for a place to worship on Sunday, April 18. There were but two choices: an evangelical Protestant service in the morning and Catholic Mass in the afternoon. With jet lag, travel weariness, and the local variant of Montezuma's revenge beginning to take their toll, we opted to rest on Sunday morning and go to the Da Nang Catholic Church that afternoon.

As our vans pulled into the square in front of the church, there must have been nearly a thousand bicycles parked side-by-side in orderly rows. Most worshipers had arrived in time for the Rosary that precedes Mass. As we stepped out of the vans, looked up, and climbed the eight steps that spanned the full length of the church's neo-gothic facade and wrapped around its sides, the bright-whiteness sparkled against the cloudy skies. The symmetrical points on either side of the central steeple seemed to join it in piercing the sky. This church was sharp contrast to the one I had walked around in Hanoi. Passing through the front doors of the Da Nang church, I was struck by how well the church was being maintained. From the magnificent window of Christ behind the altar to the rose window over the front doors, great care was in evidence for the glorification of God and His house. As I looked down the nave with its goldenrod Corinthian columns and silver caps, I realized that on one side of the main aisle the women were seated. Men sat on the other. While someone went to find the priest who was expecting our visit and most of our traveling companions looked in from the wide-opened side doors and shuttered windows that lined the sides of the church, I joined the men in one of the nearly full pews.

Only minutes before Mass was to begin, Denny Johnson, one of our team members, located the church's pastor, and I went to meet him. His name is Father Anthony Nguyen. Father Anthony wore a white cassock and a wide smile and spoke very good English, though he very definitely looked fatigued. He had graduated from seminary in Dalat, had at one point studied in Rome, and had been the sole pastor of what was an obviously enormous flock ever since his fellow priests had gone "on retreat." I naively asked him why they all were gone at once and how much longer he would be here alone. He smiled gently and said, "I do not know how much longer they will be gone. Their 'retreat' is mandatory; they have been gone a very long time."

I have often heard it said that there is no better way to shore up the church and build faith than to suffer persecution. If that is so, these Christians in Da Nang and the others we met in ones and twos elsewhere in Vietnam, are probably the best example I have ever seen.

The church was full by the time the liturgy began, and additional parishioners were seated six-deep outside the open doors under the colonnade and on the steps. Others stood in the back, looking through the doors where we had entered. All were attentive and prayerful. They sang with full voice, and their responses were crisp and sincere. Those gathered, listened closely as Father Anthony preached what seemed to be an inspiring and stirring sermon. It would have been hard to convince anyone that this congregation attended church merely out of habit. The focused, spiritual fervor in Da Nang could have made any charismatic assembly in the United States envious.

It seems inevitable that as Vietnam opens more to the West and its market economy overcomes the vestiges of communism, more and more churches will open, too. We were told stories about how difficult it had been to bring Bibles into the country; however, when we asked government officials whether we could include cases of Bibles in our shipments of medical equipment and supplies, the answer was a universal "yes." As a matter of fact, Denny Johnson had purchased thirty-two Vietnamese language Bibles in Hong Kong, and we stuffed them into our luggage. Lyn Cryderman, our photographer and editor, met a woman who identified herself as a Christian and said that she had worked for the American consulate in Da Nang until the Americans fled. He asked her if she had a Bible, and she said she did not—so he gave her one. The look of astonishment and excitement on her face stirred us all. She did not hide the black-bound book as we suspected she might but held it proudly next to her breast, as a young girl might when coming out of Sunday school.

We sensed that while the various People's Committees may not be ready to allow missionaries free reign, or permit the establishment of a Vietnamese Bible Society with its own in-country publishing arm, the days of treating religion as criminal, or as a "counter-revolutionary" activity, are over. If necessity is the mother of invention, what we may be seeing in Vietnam is a new era where the church will be renewed out of a need for a moral foundation as the country seeks to reap the fruits of a healthy economy and certain basics of subsistence. Or, at the very least, out of a desire for bandages and antibiotics, the Vietnamese people could be given the opportunity to hear the Good News.

25

TOUCHED BY WAR

___

Vietnam: 1993

THERE IS VIRTUALLY NO ONE IN VIETNAM WHOSE personal life went untouched by war, yet life goes on. Though no definitive record exists today, the officials we met with in the Hanoi government estimate that more than 1.5 million Vietnamese lost their lives and that more than three million were wounded; roughly ten percent of the population of the two nations. No one will approximate how many died in the "consolidation" of the country. More than a million have become refugees.

To make those staggering figures more understandable, it is likely that every Vietnamese alive at the time lost a loved one, or a limb, or a home. And everyone in the nation knows others who suffered the same losses.

For more than a decade the entire population of the northern half of the country was told regularly that the United States was the Asian equivalent of the "Great Satan." Tens of thousands of their young sons who were sent south to fight against us, never returned, nor were they ever heard from again.

In the southern part of the country, after ten years of American presence and promises, we abandoned the country we had said we would save. By the time the last American combat units were withdrawn from Vietnam in 1972, critics of the Republic of Vietnam were saying that their troops would not fight. Yet, in 1974 alone, the South Vietnamese military suffered 31,000 casualties. When the final collapse came, less than a month after the U.S. Congress vetoed South Vietnam's final plea for American military equipment, hundreds of thousands who had trusted us, worked for us, and fought with us were killed, forced to flee, or sent to "reeducation camps." Some, reportedly, are still there.

Yet, in spite of all this, from the northern tip of the country, south all the way to what is now Ho Chi Minh City, there is no evidence of hostility or animosity toward Americans. "We want you to come back" was the cry we heard most from the people. More than once we were told, "We love Americans." In fact, the only "danger" that Americans face in Vietnam is to be mistakenly identified as Russians. The Vietnamese very clearly don't like the Russians.

A new generation of Vietnamese children has grown up in a world in which reminders of the war are ever-present. Outside the gate of a primary school in Hanoi is a large fishpond. A B-52 bomber crashed there almost two decades before the children now attending school were born. Part of the exposed wreckage, still rising out of the pond, serves as a constant reminder of war. When we visited the site, the happy youngsters, all toothy smiles, tried out their schoolroom English on us. They did not hate the Americans who had bombed their parents.

More than six million tons of bombs were dropped on the two Vietnams during the war. Shortly after the unification of the country in 1975, the Hanoi government guessed that Vietnam had as many as twenty million bomb craters. While both numbers are disputed, Vietnam's major north-south thoroughfare, Highway 1, is a testament to the ferocity with which the American aircraft pounded North Vietnam. On either side of the road—which has been repeatedly repaired but would not qualify as a decent county lane in most American states—are ponds rimmed by the emerald green growth of a lush land. The ponds are not a part of the natural landscape. Each was hewn by the air-dropped ordnance of American bombing runs. Years later these permanent pockmarks of war have a definite beauty to them, fish and ducks have made them home. Life goes on.

War's deadly remnants continue to claim human life, however. Near Khe Sanh we saw children collecting scrap metal from the former battlefield. They do so using probes to pierce the red soil in hopes of finding a piece that will fetch a couple of cents when sold to Japanese buyers. Sometimes they come upon old grenades, U.S. and "ChiCom"; or still-armed

Soviet and American-made anti-personnel mines, or unexploded bombs, rockets, and artillery shells. All too often they explode, adding yet another name to the war's casualty list and forever changing the course of another life.

While we were there in 1993, Vietnamese officials told us that there are in all of Vietnam, over 350,000 orphans under the age of seventeen, and nearly a quarter of a million disabled veterans of the million who were wounded but had survived. Again, there is no way to confirm the claim, but on every street in every city and village there is visible evidence of an epic tragedy.

In Dong Ha I had the pleasure of meeting with a group of fellow veterans, fellow survivors of the war. All four of them—Lieutenant Colonel Le The Dahn, Lieutenant Colonel Hoang Kim Dien, Major Ta Quang Thanh, and Major Tran Thanh Toan—had fought as officers with the Viet Cong, or the North Vietnamese Army. I recount their names here as a small but proud tribute to them. We sat and talked for some time. We shared war stories. Except for the language barrier that forced us to use an interpreter, I had the sense that we could have been sitting around at a local VFW post, old warriors reminiscing and talking about the old days. I was interested in hearing about their lives and experiences. They wanted to know about mine as well. After talk of war, we spoke about our families and how proud we were of how well our wives had cared for and raised our children while we were fighting each other. Twenty-five years earlier, any one of them might have taken my life in battle, or I theirs. When we parted, we toasted our fallen comrades and then each other in gratitude that we had all survived.

Cemeteries dot the Vietnamese landscape. Vietnam must have more of them per square mile than any of the scores of countries I've visited in my lifetime. I certainly don't recall having seen as many anywhere else. At countless locations, up and down the roads, north and south, east and west, the same white monument stands in the midst of countless graves, each marked with a slab and its own incense pot. Like America's own national cemeteries, many are on the very soil where blood was shed. In many cases, the dead rest near where they fell.

But sadly, in Vietnam's veterans' cemeteries only the victors are honored. Each towering white monument bears a red hammer and sickle or a gold star on a red field. To the victors come honor and tribute. To those who failed, anonymity and disgrace. I saw not one grave or cemetery to commemorate those who had fallen for the South, and I found that to be disturbing for a nation so clearly intent on trying to heal the wounds of war.

In one of our meetings I raised this matter with our host, a member of the local People's Committee. A former soldier, now a party official, this man had asked me about how we had come together as a nation after our civil war. I told him that I am from Virginia, where much of that war had been fought, that in the Shenandoah Valley where I live, there are many battlefields, but that in each one of them, no matter the outcome of that particular battle, there were monuments and memorials to those who had fought and fallen on both sides of the conflict.

I don't know the effect of that conversation with one official of the Vietnamese government, but hopefully someone there can see the one clear parallel between those bloody events on our own soil and the great conflict in which the people of Vietnam were engaged for so long: They both united divided nations. One of the most fitting symbols of the unity that they seek to achieve in Vietnam would be to honor those who died on the other side in that struggle.

One can only wonder, once the present transition has found its inevitable end, what will be thought about the generation of Vietnamese from the South whose fathers were taken in battle without recognition. Alternatively, what will come of the innumerable cemeteries honoring those who fought for the victors? And more important for us, what role will we play from half a world away in bringing about a just future full of hope to those on whose behalf we spent the better part of a generation and nearly sixty thousand American lives?

26

BATTLEFIELDS THEN AND NOW

THE VIETNAM WAR WAS WAGED ON THOUSANDS OF battlefields. It was contested waist-deep, in manure-stinking rice paddies on misty mountain highlands, on white sand beaches, in the suffocating heat of triple-canopied jungle, on sun-bleached crests covered with flesh-tearing "razor" grass, in the muddy tributaries and surrounding waters of three seas, and in the air over four countries. Skirmishes of The War were also fought on America's city streets, college campuses, around dining room tables, and in front of the family television, in pulpits and pews, and in the corridors of political power in our nation's capital.

Nearly three million of America's sons and 11,500 of its daughters went to The War and, if they survived, had images of battle forever burned into their memories. But The War also affected

243

those who never went to Southeast Asia, who had no sons, daughters, spouses, siblings, or parents who went there; who had no connection with it other than to have its bellicose likeness blasted into their homes on television.

All of us who lived through those days in the 1960s and '70s made mental snapshots of the war, no matter how remote our vantage point. We recorded the sounds of combat and the visions of battle and the names of strange places that came with a left-right, two-syllable cadence to our tongues: *Da Nang, Chu Lai, Khe Sanh, Pleiku, Kon Tum, Dak To, Con Thien, Bien Hoa, Na Trang, Quang Tri, Dong Ha, Saigon, Hanoi*. The list is almost endless.

I am one of those who came back from those places nearly a quarter century ago with those images and sounds frozen in my mind. And though time has faded the impressions that were made then, I was not prepared for how much the places had changed in the two-and-one-half decades since I had been there. Somehow, I had imagined that it would still be the same. It wasn't.

When I returned to Vietnam in 1993, I went back to the battlefields where I had served so long ago. The changes I witnessed were dramatic and moving because they were overlaid by all those experiences I had as a young man engaged in a desperate struggle.

When I arrived in Vietnam as that young man, it was to a unit at Con Thien Combat Base, just south of the Demilitarized Zone to which I was assigned.

Then, this barren, red-clay hilltop with its rabbit warren of buried bunkers, miles of barbed wire, minefields, and high observation towers, was barely suited for human habitation, though we lived there. It was at Con Thien that I had watched Bud Flowers, our artillery forward observer, climb one of those towers in the midst of a furious barrage of NVA rocket fire so that he could call in our own fire power in response.

It was at Con Thien that I first saw men killed as they ate or slept, just because they were at the wrong place at the wrong time. It was there that I first smelled the awful stench of human excrement being disposed of in the only way we could in bases like these—by burning it in halved fifty-five gallon drums filled with diesel fuel. And it was in the much bombed and blasted areas around Con Thien, in "Leatherneck Square" and on "Mutter's Ridge," that I came to know courageous men and those who led them.

Perhaps my clearest memory of Con Thien is of the many young Marines I knew who were wounded or killed in its vicinity. It was within sight of this stark hilltop that Les Shafer, Mike Wunsch, and Frank Coulombe were killed and I was hurt on three separate occasions. And we had plenty of company. First Platoon's Bill Haskell, badly wounded in May '69, was replaced by Eric Bowen, who in turn was wounded. When 3d Platoon's Rich O'Neill left, his place was taken by Ross Petersen who was wounded within weeks. Art Vandaveer, who replaced Bud Flowers, was nearly killed west of Con Thien firebase.

It was with those memories that I returned to

Con Thien in 1993. I was unprepared for how much it had changed in my absence.

The watchtowers and bunkers are now all gone. The barbed wire has been scavenged for scrap. And though mines and "dud" ordnance are still in the ground, the soil around the still-bald hilltop is now tilled and under cultivation. Pineapples, tea, eucalyptus and rubber trees now cover the terrain that I had once patrolled so carefully. Had I not recognized the distinctive, raised, flat profile of the firebase, I would have been hard-pressed to believe that I was standing where my old battalion once had its forward headquarters.

In 1968–69 our battalion's "rear" area had been located in Quang Tri. Then it was a bustling, riverside, provincial capital, beyond the range of North Vietnam's big guns and rockets, and famous for its historic citadel.

The province I had walked over so much of in the 1960s still bears the name *Quang Tri*, but the city I had known is no more. Quang Tri was overrun and virtually destroyed in the Easter 1972 NVA offensive that presaged the fall of South Vietnam. The fifteen-foot stone walls of the fifty-acre citadel are now nearly all leveled, and the former city is but a shadow of its former prominence. Driving along Highway 1 in the Spring of '93, I had a hard time convincing my companions that we were in the midst of what was once the largest population center in what had been northern South Vietnam.

Northwest of what's left of Quang Tri City is Dong Ha. It was here that I and so many others, shattered on the battlefield, had been taken by helicopter for medical care. Then, Dong Ha was a small village, notable because it had an airfield operated by the Marines and a concrete-and-steel bunker complex buried deep underground, that served as the 3d Marine Division's headquarters. In those days, Dong Ha was really little more than a military base and a small local village. During the 1972 NVA offensive that overran Quang Tri Province, John Ripley, a Marine advisor with the South Vietnamese Marines, had earned the Navy Cross for heroically blowing up the Dong Ha bridge across the nearby river.

Today Dong Ha is the capital of Quang Tri Province and while not a modern city by any standard, it has a flurry of activity and commerce about it—people getting things done. The marketplace in the center of the city is replete with every form of enterprise and entrepreneurship imaginable—and the people are full of remarkably friendly smiles for American visitors. To offset our pathetic, Russian-built accommodations—the best in town—we found a restaurant that, though rustic, did cook up a delicious dish of squid.

Once the sight of the most famous "siege" in all the Vietnam war, the Khe Sanh of 1993 is a plateau surrounded by verdant hills. Seeing it again, so dramatically changed, was a shock to me. In 1969, my platoon had occupied an observation post on Hill 950 overlooking the Marine Combat base that had been built and held with so much American blood. When I had looked down on Khe Sanh from that windy hilltop, everything outside the base perimeter was desolation. The land had been stripped nearly bare of foliage by the instruments of war.

The so-called 75-day siege of Khe Sanh was over before I got to Vietnam. By the time I occupied the lonely hilltop north of the base, there were only reminders of the five infantry battalions that had occupied it and fought so tenaciously on the surrounding hills. The miles of barbed wire, sandbagged revetments, and handful of concrete bunkers were still there. So, too, was its steel-matted airstrip, which had been the key to replenishing the six thousand Marines committed to Khe San.

I had still been a midshipman at Annapolis, watching The War on television, as the February 5, 1968, North Vietnamese attack on Hill 861 to the west was repulsed by the Marines. On both my 1969 and 1993 trips to Khe Sanh, I could vividly recall news of the NVA armor assault that overran the U.S. Army Special Forces base at Lang Vei, just to the south of the base. On my 1993 return, we followed the same route to Khe Sanh that had been used by the joint U.S. Army, ARVN, and Marine relief column during OPERATION PEGASUS.

By the time I got to Vietnam in late 1968, I was well aware that the battle for Khe Sanh was never quite as desperate as it had been portrayed in the newspapers and on television at home. The total U.S. Marine and U.S. Army casualty count, including OPERATION PEGASUS, was 199 killed and 830 wounded.

On the old battlefield today there is a stone memorial marker, placed there by the Hanoi government. Almost sheepishly, one of our "guides" read to us the extraordinary claims engraved upon it: *10,000 Imperialist Marines killed in action, hundreds of planes shot down, thousands more "puppet" troops (South Vietnamese) killed and routed.* After reading these preposterous assertions, he turned and said with a smile, "I'm only translating what it says."

Despite the propaganda, there is no doubt that Khe Sanh was a terrible battle for those who fought in it—on both sides. When I had asked about it in Hanoi, one of our escorts admitted that four NVA infantry divisions, reinforced by two artillery regiments and armored units—forty thousand men in all—had attacked the Khe Sanh Combat Base. And while our own official estimates of NVA casualties vary widely, from 1000 confirmed killed to 8000 – 10,000 estimated wounded, the Hanoi government maintains that they really do not know how many of their own they lost there.

Though it was abandoned over two decades ago, the distinctive imprint remains still of the airstrip where C-130s "skid-dropped" and parachuted supplies and ammunition. Brush has grown up all around, and the revetments are long gone, but there is no mistaking the runway's 3000-foot outline in the red latterite soil on which nothing grows.

In early 1969, Major General Ray Davis, then the commanding general of the 3d Marine Division, ordered two regiments down the Dakrong River Valley and into the deep jungle slopes of the A Shau on OPERATION DEWEY CANYON. My platoon was sent to hold Hill 950 and to keep an eye on the Khe Sanh plateau to the south of the mountains we occupied. General Davis, a Marine hero from Korea, believed that all the bad press that Khe Sanh had received months earlier was undeserved. He flew in the 3d Marine Division Band and held a colors ceremony on the runway, defying the North Vietnamese Army gunners to open fire. When no NVA rounds came screaming in, those of us who watched the ceremony concluded that the enemy forward observers, seeing this remarkable display of bravado, probably were disbelieved when they made their frantic calls for artillery-fire missions. We could almost hear the responses from the NVA artillery and rocket battery commanders: "Sure, Nguyen, we heard you say there's a parade at Khe Sanh. Do us a favor, will you? Lay off the opium!"

Between Dong Ha and Khe Sanh is The Rockpile—one of the least changed of all the sites I knew from my year in Vietnam in the 1960s. Only the passing of the geological ages will refashion this massive, natural pile of boulders that juts up nearly 700 feet and that once was the headquarters of my regiment, the 3d Marines. When I last saw it, American radio antennas bristled like long whiskers across its summit. Marine forward observers and lookouts with powerful night-vision scopes had covered its crest, and at its base was a major artillery emplacement. Those of us who had to scale it dreaded the task. It took the combined skills of pack animal, mountain goat, and rock ape—and a good two hours to climb to the top.

Today, looking up from its base, there is something almost pristine about it. Though The Rockpile is still an imposing feature of the terrain, there are today no signs of our ever having been there. When we Marines abandoned the site, it must have been taken over by Vietnam's own native rock apes.

From The Rockpile I could see in the distance places that are etched deeply in my memory and from which I still bear the scars today. A few thousand meters north is "The Razorback"—named by Marines who had preceded me to Vietnam—in recognition of the distinctive and precipitous features in its terrain. Farther north is Mutter's Ridge and what was once the southern border of the long-gone DMZ—that line marked on our maps that had been recognized and honored only by our side in the war.

As I stood near The Rockpile, pointing out these mountainous ridgelines to my companions in 1993, each hill evoked recollections of particular events, of people, tragedies, and triumphs that I had lived through long ago. Seeing them again brought back bittersweet memories of men whom I was once closer to than any I have since known.

The positions we had occupied on central Vietnam's hilltops and ridgelines are still marked on the old terrain maps that I used as a young lieutenant. Wherever we went, we Americans always wanted to seize and hold the "high" ground. That pursuit is part of conventional wisdom in military tactics and part philosophy of life.

The Vietnamese, never an adversary to take lightly, took a different approach. Tenacious, committed, wily, and competent, the North Vietnamese and Viet Cong forces we faced took advantage of the high ground when they could—but settled for going underground when necessary.

I saw only a few of their underground facilities when I was a Marine. The most impressive of these were inside the DMZ, where they built their bases with relative assurance that, aside from an occasional bomb or artillery round, they would not be assaulted. While I was leading my platoon in 1968 – 69, we often wondered what it was like for them, how they lived, north of what we called the DMZ. The area was regularly pounded by U.S. aircraft, and along the coast was punished by naval gunfire from our ships in the South China Sea. But it was not until my 1993 trip to Vietnam that I had the opportunity to learn firsthand how the Vietnamese were able to so effectively evade us, so miraculously survive our air-dropped bombs and heavy naval gunfire, and yet so suddenly resurface to cause us harm. I was fascinated with what I saw under the bluffs near the sandy South China Sea beach at Vinh Moc.

At the height of The War, Vinh Moc's miles and miles of crisscrossing tunnels, many of them not even high enough for an American to stand in, most of them the equivalent of three or four stories below ground, literally became a subterranean home to thousands of Vietnamese. Alcoves were cut out of the underground pathways to serve as family dens and, we were told, babies had been born there. Multiple, well-hidden entrances allowed NVA soldiers on the way south and the local populace to descend into this dark, dank but well-protected world.

During our 1993 visit to this underground village

complex, I learned quickly that this would not have been my kind of war. A nagging claustrophobia closed in around me as we entered the hand-dug, musty, damp, and stuffy accommodations. When we came back to the surface, our hosts took us to the museum they had built above the tunnels as a memorial to the ingenuity and persistence of those who had dug them, lived in them, and emerged from them to fight elsewhere. As I exited the tunnels, one of the Vietnamese who had accompanied us, a former NVA soldier, asked me if I would make a notation in their tattered "guest book." I wrote: "From a soldier to a former enemy: I admire your courage, perseverance, and tenacity. Thank you for showing me what we were up against."

27

GOING HOME

Vietnam: 1969, 1993

LEAVING VIETNAM IN 1969, THOUGH NOT SPEEDY, was a relatively hassle-free process.

Our transfer orders, medical records, and baggage were checked. A Navy chief lectured everyone in the waiting area of the Da Nang Movement Center on the need to keep taking our anti-malaria medicine. A very large provost marshal with an MP arm band allowed each departing soldier, sailor, airman, or Marine, to pass through a small, curtained "amnesty booth" where items like live ammunition, hand grenades, captured enemy weapons, and other such contraband could be placed in a large bin, no questions asked, before our bags were run through the final security search. The bureaucratic, hurry-up-and-wait, red-tape routine, so typical of the military, would have resulted in profane complaints anywhere else. But we were a docile, compliant crowd in fairly patient good humor. After all, we were going home!

Our departure in 1993 was distinctly different. We arrived at the airport directly from the 1000-bed, Japanese-built Cho Ray Hospital, Saigon's biggest medical facility and the most modern in all of Vietnam. Stepping out of minivans, our group of a dozen Americans, some loaded down with souvenirs wrapped in brown paper in addition to garment bags, suitcases, lap top computers, and a variety of television production gear, looked like a herd of pack animals. We quickly found ourselves in a long line of similarly laden baggage rats, each waiting his turn for the first test of will — the end goal of which was to make it through Vietnam's final bureaucratic maze.

In typical Communist fashion, the Saigon airport is a minefield of bureaucratic hassles designed to bring fear to even the toughest, nerves-of-steel traveler. While there may well be malevolent motives for making things so difficult, I've decided that the real purpose behind having so many echelons of people standing around in a variety of uniforms, giving the appearance of utter seriousness, is really quite simple: the creation of jobs! And infinite layers of bureaucracy make lots of jobs.

First is the "ticket checker." Only one of these, for the hundreds of hopefuls in the sweating throng. His job is to ensure that each soul, dragging his or her bags along a foot or so at a time, does indeed have a ticket entitling the bearer to travel to some destination away from Vietnam.

Next, a "passport checker," whose task it is to carefully scrutinize the terrible photo glued inside the blue folder for any resemblance to the harried traveler standing in front of him. First he glances at me, then at the photo. Then at me. Then, once again, at the photo. I make an effort to look as much like the younger me in the photograph as possible. I don't want to be left behind for lack of looking like myself. It suddenly occurs to me, as this noble lord of Lenin is peering back and forth at me and my passport, why they tell you not to smile when having your passport photo taken. It's because you cannot possibly duplicate that joyful grin, standing in a 120-degree room with sweat dripping off your nose, holding 150 pounds of baggage in aching hands, while an inscrutable passport checker assesses the shape of your ear lobes. He shrugs as if to suggest the hopelessness of my appearance, hands me back my passport, and dismisses me with a derisive wave to the next test—the "visa checker."

There are two of these elevated authorities—choose your fate. I take what appears to be the shorter, thus I think the faster, of the two queues. I am wrong. Neither line is moving. It is apparently the job of the two visa checkers to determine whether the person standing in front of him is actually there—that he or she had permission to enter the country he or she now wishes to leave. He apparently starts this essential process by carefully comparing the spelling of the name in your passport and the way it is inscribed on your Entry Visa—a document issued months before by someone I have never met in Ottawa, Canada, whose barely legible handwriting is now the key to my future. Periodically, the visa checker consults some document below the counter as he slowly moves his finger down the entries on the visa. I hold my breath as he reaches for the stamp, scowls at me one more time and then, with a sweeping flourish that would make any conductor of the New York Philharmonic proud, proceeds to administer several death-dealing blows with his rubber stamp to the piece of paper before him. Ah, sweet victory. "On to customs!"

At this juncture it became apparent to all of us that being the customs official marks the height of success for a worthy son or daughter of Marx. There are dozens of them. One can immediately tell that these are the top of the bureaucratic totem pole in Saigon. They each have their own chair. There is even a table to lean on. They know that they have you in their power. And they love it! The old Delta Airlines slogan races giddily through my mind: "We're Delta. We love flying, and it shows." Only here it's "We're Customs. We love hassles, and it shows."

Most of us were bound for home via Bangkok and Tokyo, but two of our video crew, Peter Larson and Heinz Fussle, had headed for other destinations and therefore had departed several hours before us. The fact that they were not still standing in one of these airport lines gave me hope that we, too, might yet get aboard an airplane and fly away. In Peter's carry-on bags were twenty-five of the fifty videotapes we had shot. The remaining tapes were in Dave Anderson's hand-carry bags, to be taken out through Bangkok. Or so we thought. Unfortunately, we had underestimated the willingness of these esteemed authorities at customs to be more than just a minor inconvenience.

The customs agent at the counter demanded that Dave produce the document that had allowed us to bring the video tapes into the country when we arrived. Dave produced the document, showing that we had brought in fifty tapes, all blank. And that's when the fun began. We didn't have fifty tapes, we only had twenty-five, and they were no longer blank—they had been recorded on. "We have a problem," was all the uniformed young man said. It was obvious to him that these untrustworthy Americans were trying to take out of Vietnam something different from what they had brought in, a flagrant violation of People's Order something-or-other.

A hasty conference ensued between the young man at the counter and the young woman seated at the desk immediately behind him. She in turn got up to confer with the older gentleman seated at a larger desk behind her. In turn, each of the potentates came to the counter, where we would repeatedly explain that the first twenty-five tapes had already gone and that it was clearly the purpose of the television cameras, also listed on the customs document, to record on the tapes.

Ah, but that's not what it said on the documents issued in Ottawa, Canada, so many weeks ago. This in turn precipitated a major negotiation with His Highest Omnipotence, the gentleman in the gray Ho Chi Minh suit at the large wooden desk at the back of the room. He slowly made his way to us, stood, and listened as we made our explanation for what seemed like the twentieth time. At the end of our plaintive soliloquy he gave his judgment: "You go, tapes stay! We will send to you later."

This decision was rendered about five minutes before the doors on our flight were about to close. We could not afford to get separated from the tapes. The recordings we had made represented the investment of several months' worth of work and hundreds of thousands of dollars. If we left the tapes in Saigon, we might never see them again. But more than money was involved. While we were in the South, we had recorded two very frank and revealing interviews with former South Vietnamese military veterans who had survived the reeducation camps. And while we thought we had carefully protected their identities, I was very concerned that if these recently released prisoners could be identified they would be in great jeopardy.

His Omnipotence would accept no appeals to his decision, leaving us but one choice: leave someone behind and hope to get the tapes out on a later flight. With the aid of a helpful Air France official, we booked Joel Samy for departure the next day, and as we ran for our gate, Joel grabbed the tapes off the counter and headed, almost as fast, for the door to the street.

As we parted, my one instruction to Joel was, "Whatever you do, don't let the tapes out of your sight. If they get their hands on them, we will never see them again."

Were they just waiting for us at the airport, hoping to seize our tapes? Had the governmental winds of favor shifted as a result of the secret police reports about our activities? Had they learned about our interviews with the reeducation camp survivors? Had they misunderstood what I meant when I said: "This is a war that can still be won, not with bombs and bullets but with band-aids and antibiotics"? Perhaps, and this was not at all unlikely, some diligent customs official in the South, defiantly ignoring the authorization from Hanoi and simply following local orders to impound all videotapes, was just doing what he thought was "a good job." Most likely, we will never know. Certainly at that moment we did not care. We just wanted to be sure that the *One More Mission* video project was not ruined.

It was hard for the rest of to us bid Joel farewell. He had worked diligently, long and hard, every day throughout the trip, trying to accommodate everyone's needs in an impossible job. There were spur-of-the-moment schedule changes, long nights and early mornings every day and, just as it seemed that his job was finished, he was left alone and quite literally, holding the bag. It was not easy boarding the plane without those tapes. But it was even harder boarding without Joel.

Joel did make it back to the States, with the tapes—not something we were entirely certain would happen. Though he has lived in the U.S. for most of his life, Joel Samy (who is of Asian-Indian extraction) carries a passport from his native Fiji. That might have been to his benefit, but it's impossible to tell. When he got out, he brought the tapes to my office in Virginia and related the rest of the story. Here is what happened:

Joel booked a room in a local hotel and got together with Michael Viola Vu (a Vietnamese-born American citizen who had been adopted as an orphan after he was evacuated from Vietnam in the 1975 "Baby Lift") to plan their strategy. They decided to solicit help from some high-powered officials who had helped us get around in Vietnam, but that turned out to be futile. When they went to customs headquarters the next day with the official, they discovered what Joel refers to as "the mother of all bureaucracies." After forty-five minutes of haggling, the verdict was rendered: The tapes wouldn't leave the country until a customs official reviewed them, and that could take two weeks.

Michael and Joel made a futile effort to track down someone who could help them but continued to have doors closed in their faces. By now they were getting desperate. It was 11:00 o'clock in the morning, and Joel had a 1:30 flight to take him and the tapes back to the U.S., but it looked as though the tapes wouldn't make it.

Then Joel had an inspiration: "Go to the airport." Call it an inner voice, God's leading, or an act of desperation, but Joel obeyed. Despite knowing that he didn't have the proper documentation to take the tapes out of the country and knowing that he risked arrest if the customs officials caught him and wanted to make an issue of it, he nonetheless headed straight for the airport. In the parking lot, he and Michael prayed the prayer that Brother Andrew prayed during the years that he smuggled Bibles into Eastern Europe: "God, please blind their eyes. Let them not see Your work."

He got out of the car, walked into the airport, went through the routine of tickets, visas, and travel documents. Then, the moment of truth arrived. The same customs officials who had given us such a hard time the day before were at their posts. Joel headed straight for them. He handed them his passport. It was stamped without question. Then he placed his bags, including the one filled with tapes, on the X-ray machine's conveyor belt. The man watching the monitor made no move whatsoever as the tapes passed through the machine. He had to have seen them, and he knew that they had not been cleared to leave the country, but he never said a word. Joel grabbed his bags and went to his plane, struggling not to let his mix of relief and anxiety show..

As soon as his plane landed in San Francisco the next morning, I received a call. Joel's voice broke the daylong tension. His report: "Mission accomplished."

To say that I was relieved is an understatement. Getting the tapes out of Vietnam was certainly important to us, but Joel's own freedom, safety, and well-being were even more so. I thanked him, congratulated him, and then hung up the phone with a brief prayer of thanks. While Joel's escape with the tapes wasn't violent, or bloody like a firefight, I once again had been blessed to witness courage, love, and faithfulness.

Our trip back to Vietnam was over, but "one more mission" was actually just beginning.

PART III

THE MISSION

28

STARTING OVER

Virginia: 1989, 1993

FOR ME, STARTING OVER IS BECOMING A WAY OF LIFE. At least it seems that way. In 1970, when I returned from my first trip to Vietnam, I had to start a new phase of my career as well as learn how to become a father. In 1975 I had to start over in my marriage after I had let it nearly come apart. In 1981, when I was ordered to the White House for duty with the National Security Council Staff, I had to learn how to work in the arcane environment of Washington power politics, diplomacy, and covert operations. And in 1989, I had to start a whole new career after retiring from the Marines.

This last transition was a bit more dramatic, and much more visible than those that preceded it. It followed a very publicized congressional inquisition in 1987 and a succession of trials and tribunals that cost millions in legal and security expenses.

As I begin again by starting a small business, I thought that Vietnam was all behind me. Little did I know then how much closer it would become in the months ahead.

All "new beginnings" bring some of the past with them. My fresh start in business was no exception. I began with a friend from my days at the White House: Joe Fernandez, one of the very few people from my days at the National Security Staff with whom I am still in contact. He had been a clandestine services officer at the CIA for more than twenty years. In other words, he was a spy for the United States. Joe's final assignment had been as the Station Chief in San Jose, Costa Rica, a position that had put him in touch with many of the refugees fleeing the Communist regime in neighboring Nicaragua.

By 1989 Joe and I were both a bit like refugees—refugees from more than two decades of government service and almost as much in need of employment as refugees who fled to this country.

We set a few very simple goals: We wanted to make something; we wanted to make something new—or at least make it better than anyone else had ever made it before; we wanted to have fun doing it; we wanted to make a profit!

After the congressional Iran-Contra hearings, the *Wall Street Journal* published the results of a little poll they had run among some of America's largest companies as to whether or not they would hire a person of my increasingly colorful background. Though there were certainly dissenters, most of the respondents had said they would. But when I started to check around, there were two things that made the offers I received unacceptable. First, all of them required a move from Virginia—something neither Betsy nor I wanted to put our children through again.

But more important was what these potential employers wanted me to do: nothing. On two occasions, I asked interviewers, "What is it that I would *do*?" The answer: "Well you would just be here, to help close deals." "What would I make?" I inquired. "Money," I was told.

Okay, I thought, *God knows my family and I need that*. But I also wanted to be able to point to *something* at the end of a work day and be able to say, "Because I was here, we made more of them," or "we made these better."

There just didn't seem to be any of *those* kinds of jobs available.

One afternoon, shortly after the legal storms had passed for both of us, Joe and I were talking about the frustration we were both feeling. On Joe's desk was a newspaper open to a story criticizing the Bush administration's efforts to stem the flow of drugs into the U.S. from Colombia. It was something I could see firsthand every day in Washington. Police were clearly losing a day-to-day battle on the streets and in the drug-saturated neighborhoods of our nation's capital.

I had been involved with SAFe, a drug-prevention program in Washington. But there was clearly more to winning the drug war than trying to keep kids from using and dealing drugs. Before he joined the CIA in the 1960s, Joe had been a police officer in Dade County, Florida. He was concerned about the law-enforcement officers out on the streets.

Joe said, "We ought to find a way to help these guys. The work you're doing at SAFe will have some long-term effect on the demand side of the equation, but the DEA, the cops, even the FBI, are hopelessly outgunned in trying to deal with the supply side of this stuff. They don't even have decent body armor."

And then, as if saying those words had thrown an electric switch in his chair, Joe bolted upright.

"That's it!" exclaimed Joe. "We can make a better body armor. If we work at it, we can find a way to make a better product than anyone has ever seen before—and sell it to the people who really need it!"

Some people believe in luck. Some believe in coincidence. Others believe that things just kind of "happen." I don't. I believe that the good Lord always watches over His children. Theologians call it Divine Providence.

And so it was that, a short while after Joe and I discussed making protective equipment for cops, I "happened" to have a conversation with General P. X. Kelley, the recently retired Commandant of the Marine Corps. He had been appointed to the board of Allied Signal, a large corporation that, he said, was developing a new material for soft armor.

General Kelley introduced us to the management of Allied Signal. We visited their production facilities and learned what we would need to get into the business. They in turn introduced us to an armor company that was looking for a buyer, and so we started building our business: Guardian

Technologies International, Inc., The Life-Saving Company.

I could write another whole book about what it's like to start your own business—the thrill of entrepreneurship, the disappointment when the deal we thought we had made with the company we were going to buy out fell through, and the determination to start up anyway.

There is enormous satisfaction in creating good jobs for good people and real pleasure in making a product that is truly superior. There is also the anxiety of meeting a payroll on a month when sales are down.

We borrowed some money, found investors for what we couldn't borrow, and set out to try to save some lives. When the company we had set out to buy decided not to sell, Providence struck again. One of that company's most experienced workers contacted Joe and me to see if we would hire her. She knew the business of making body armor and she knew a whole lot about starting over. She was a refugee from communism and the long-ago war in Southeast Asia I thought I had put behind me. Her name is Bouakeo Bounkong, and we couldn't have started over without her.

Bouakeo began to recruit workers for us from among her fellow refugees. In a matter of weeks we were training a work force and developing our own products. We spent a small fortune on testing, evaluation, research, development, design work, and patent filings. And before we could sell anything to American law enforcement, we had to complete the lengthy and expensive process of having our new equipment certified by the National

Institute of Justice, the federal agency that sets performance standards for protective equipment like ours.

Most of our new employees, almost overnight, were refugees from the Vietnam War. Few spoke any English. We were concerned about their ability to understand the complex rules, regulations, and certification requirements we were faced with, so we decided to take some of our scarce capital and hire a teacher who could come in at the end of the day to teach them English. Not only would this help our company, we reasoned, but it would also ease our employees' transition into American society.

I thought the teacher we hired was perfect for the task. She was a high school ESL teacher (English as a Second Language), board-certified in one of the finest school systems in the country and had been at it since shortly after she arrived in the U.S. as a refugee herself. Best of all, I thought, she, too, was from Vietnam.

She hadn't been there an hour on her first day when Bouakeo appeared at my door. "We no more want this teacher," Bouakeo said.

"Why, Bouakeo, she's perfect for the job. If someone doesn't understand what she's saying in English, they can ask her in Vietnamese," I replied.

"You not understand," she responded in her broken English. "We want to learn English from somebody who was born here. That way we not learn English with a Vietnamese accent."

That bittersweet exchange taught me a valuable lesson about how much those of us who are born here take for granted. It struck me that what Bouakeo and her co-workers wanted more than anything else was simply to be "Americans." They did not want to be hyphenated Vietnamese-Americans or Asian-Americans. They just wanted to be Americans. They came here to make new lives for themselves. They weren't ashamed of where they had come from, but they were here to start over. They wanted the opportunity to be fully accepted as Americans. Nothing more. Nothing less.

America is mostly made up of people who came here to make better lives for themselves. And certainly, not all immigrants came as refugees. But whether refugees or immigrants, those arriving in America have typically seen this land as a place of opportunity where industry and hard work are rewarded.

The work ethic of Bouakeo and her team, who actually make the soft body armor we sell, has made Guardian Technologies the success that it is. We started with nothing but an idea, but that's not enough to compete in the marketplace. Capitalism rewards the best product at the best price and also rewards the worker who is most diligent and productive. Critics of capitalism who say it exploits workers are really criticizing greed, something that is not unknown in socialist and Communist systems as well. Bouakeo and her crew are well paid, but they also work hard so that police and military personnel around the world can depend on the armor they buy from Guardian. It is almost poetic that people who came to this country to make new lives for themselves are making equipment that helps save lives.

From our very first days at Guardian, Joe and I agreed that those who help us make our innovative products should receive the recognition they deserve. So we put Bouakeo's name, along with Joe Fernandez's and mine, on our patent applications for our advanced technology flexible armor. For as long as the U.S. Patent Office remains in existence, Bouakeo's name will be memorialized as a tribute to the work she has done to help save the lives of American police officers.

Watching our employees succeed is about as good as it gets for a Vietnam vet like me, and it is especially satisfying to watch as our refugee-employees, both native-born and immigrant American, build new lives for themselves. When Bouakeo and her husband came to the United States, all they had was hope. They left everything behind and arrived at Washington National Airport with nothing but the clothes on their backs and their four children in tow. The day was November 7, 1975.

At her husband's insistence, Bouakeo stayed home with the children until their youngest entered kindergarten in 1978. Her husband got a job for $3.50 an hour in a gas station and worked more than twelve hours a day, six days a week, to support his family. He went on to work two jobs, one at night from 11:00 P.M. until 7:00 in the morning, and another day job so that he could save enough money to buy a house.

I asked Bouakeo's daughter—their oldest child, also called Bo—about her coming to America. She was in first grade in 1975 and has come a long way since that first autumn day here.

I remember when I first came over just realizing how fortunate the kids are here, with their sneakers and backpacks and things like that. We didn't have anything except the Salvation Army clothing and anything that was donated to us. I suppose the best thing from day-to-day is just to have a full meal—a lunch and a dinner. So for us to get clothing and have a chance to go to school were great pluses for us.

A lot of Americans don't realize the freedom that they have here—the freedom to travel anywhere without having an official follow you or having someone monitor your travel. But the biggest part is the opportunity that Americans have here in the United States. The only limitations here are the limitations we place on ourselves.

Like the children of immigrants in the past, Bo has worked hard. She worked her way through school and has an undergraduate degree in industrial engineering and operations research. Currently, she's finishing up her master's thesis while holding down a full-time job. She plans to go to law school. On the side, she's started a sewing company to provide jobs for *other* new immigrants.

I know that I am very fortunate to be in the position that I am in right now. When we came here it was such a big shock. We literally had nothing. I remember those days, so I want to be able to help these people who are just coming over and starting fresh. I want to give them the opportunity to help themselves and hopefully build something to contribute to the American society that has given us so much.

You might think these are the words of an idealistic young woman. They are. But she is no mere dreamer. Yes, she has spent most of her life at school. But while she was learning, she has also been working. Before her sixteenth birthday she had her first sales job in a local clothing store. She worked part-time while in college at Virginia Tech. Today, she is a patent examiner at the U.S. Patent and Trademark Office, a part of the Department of Commerce.

Her mother had never mentioned to Bo our Guardian Technologies' body armor patents. One day at work, just out of curiosity, Bo typed the name Bouakeo into the computer to see if there were any inventors with that name. She was astonished to find her mother's name listed on one of our applications for a U.S. Patent.

"I am very proud of my mom. And I'm proud of the work she's doing. It goes back to what I said before. The opportunities here are tremendous."

Whenever I'm tempted to feel sorry for myself because I've had to start over a few times, I think of Bouakeo and her family. All of us who fought in Vietnam were fighting for an idea. We had hoped our year or so "in country" would help make that country safe, its people free to live happy, productive lives. It didn't happen that way, but with the grace of the good Lord I have been fortunate to be able to give a few Vietnamese the chance to prosper.

Now I think it's time to go back and finish what we started over there.

29

SEMPER FIDELIS

Virginia: Christmas, 1990

SHORTLY AFTER WE OPENED THE DOORS OF GUARDIAN Technologies International, in the summer of 1990, the Persian Gulf War started and our once-quiet phones suddenly began ringing off the hook. For me this was a blessed relief, not just because we were getting orders, but because all the work served to distract me from what I missed—being with Marines. And though I didn't realize it at the time, it also helped plant the seeds of an idea about how Americans could turn the tragedy of Vietnam into something positive.

Like most Americans, I watched the news as Desert Shield became Desert Storm. Every broadcast was full of names and faces I knew well. Had we not been up to our armpits trying to meet a

275

very tough production schedule, it would have hurt terribly to be staying home while others got to lead Marines in harm's way.

As the buildup in Saudi Arabia proceeded, many of my old comrades-in-arms flooded my mailbox with "letters from the front." Their stories were typical and remarkably reminiscent of days long gone. Too much sun, too little sunscreen. Boot laces that soon eroded with the sweat and sand. The lack of everything—from eyewash to purge the desert dust out of red eyes to toothpaste to get the grit out of dry mouths.

Late one evening in October, I was leaving from the airport in Louisville, Kentucky, when a young Army major approached me. He said that he was from a South Dakota National Guard unit that was deploying that night to Saudi Arabia. Pointing to a group of 100 soldiers dressed in desert camouflage garb with their packs, weapons, helmets, and flak jackets, gathered beside a U.S. Air Force C-141 cargo plane, he said, "Sir, would you please come down to the flight line and say good-bye to my troops. It would mean a lot to them."

I noticed a TV news crew taping the troops under bright lights beside the terminal.

"Major," I said, sensitive to the controversy that still followed me, "see that news camera there?" He nodded.

"If they film me saying good-bye to your soldiers and someone in Washington sees that film, you're liable to find yourself in very hot water."

"Colonel North," he replied, "three weeks ago I was going to work in the morning and going home to my family at night. Now, those same folks in

Washington have seen fit to shave my head and send me to Saudi Arabia to work. I won't get to go home for months. What else can they do to me?"

I went and said good-bye to his troops. Later that night on my flight back home I was overwhelmed by it all. This was the first time I had been with that many young people, in that kind of clothing, next to that kind of aircraft, headed for that kind of a place, and that I wasn't going with them!

At home later that night I turned on the news. Sadly, much of it was dedicated to the new antiwar movement that was protesting the coalition buildup of forces in Saudi Arabia.

Several months before, with the encouragement of Rich DeVos, the head of Amway, I had started an educational and charitable foundation called the Freedom Alliance. Our fledgling efforts were serious and had gained strong support. I was doing a daily radio commentary, publishing a monthly newsletter, and holding an occasional seminar encouraging people to get involved in the public policy process.

The morning after I got back to my offices in Virginia from the Kentucky trip where I'd said good-bye to those troops on the tarmac, I called in Freedom Alliance's small staff and described the emotional farewell I'd had the night before in Louisville. I recalled for them how I had felt in Vietnam when the news from home was full of protests and anger. I told them I wanted to do something to show our troops in Saudi Arabia that the protesters and the media didn't truly represent the real sentiments of the American people. The Freedom Alliance staff sprang into action.

Within a matter of weeks this small team, headed by retired Marine Lieutenant General Ed Bronars, once my Division Commander, put together and shipped over 120,000 Christmas presents—worth nearly $3 million—to the troops in the desert. It was a great example of what Rich DeVos calls "compassionate capitalism."

By the time Desert Storm was over, we had not only sent two enormous shipments of "care" packages, but had instituted a program to help families visit their wounded soldiers, sailors, airmen, and Marines. And later on, after receiving a particularly moving letter from a new widow, we started a scholarship program for the dependents of those who were killed in this remarkably brief war.

It was only afterward that I realized that my actions in 1990, during a war that some said would "put the Vietnam Syndrome" behind us, were in large part driven by my memories of the Vietnam War. The Persian Gulf conflict stirred those long-stilled images of that place I had fought in so long ago. There was no escaping the fact that Vietnam was still much on the minds of many. Some of those who were out protesting the Persian Gulf War were the old hands from the Vietnam days. And in my work with Guardian, the aftermath of Vietnam was daily in front of me as more than a dozen refugees from that faraway, long ago war arrived each day to make life-protecting equipment for Americans in danger. Though I could not see nor sense it at the time, the ground was being broken for one more mission back to Vietnam.

30

MISSIONS OF HOPE

Vietnam: 1993

WHEN GENERAL JOHN VESSEY RETURNED FROM HIS
first trip to Vietnam in 1987 as President Reagan's
special envoy to Hanoi, he urged that U.S.-based
relief organizations get involved in providing
humanitarian help to the people of Vietnam. Soon
dozens of organizations were engaged in this effort.

For those first few nongovernmental organizations, or NGOs, it wasn't easy to get started.
Permissions had to be obtained from both the U.S.
and the Vietnamese governments, and because travel to Vietnam had been banned for U.S. citizens for
so long, special flight arrangements had to be made.

Two of the earliest American groups to be
approved for operating in Vietnam were International
Aid and Vets with a Mission. While there are today

279

more than 150 such humanitarian groups approved for operation in Vietnam, I've focused on these two because I'm familiar with their work and the hope they offer for healing in both Vietnam *and* America. Both organizations went to Vietnam in response to General Vessey's initiative, and both offer hope for the future regardless of the outcome of the "normalization" discussions between Washington and Hanoi.

International Aid became involved again in Vietnam in 1988. Like many of the NGOs, they served there before the fall of Saigon in 1975. Ralph Plumb, the president and CEO of International Aid, had been a chaplain in the U.S. Navy Reserve, and, though he had not served in Vietnam, he did spend considerable time with others in the Naval Service who had.

The Navy has special duty assignments for doctors and chaplains who are particularly hardheaded. They send them to minister and tend to Marines. It was while Ralph was on duty with Marine aviators at El Toro, California, that he was moved to see what he could do to help the healing process for Vietnam. I asked Ralph what motivated him to get involved in this war that for many veterans has never really ended.

As a chaplain, I met dozens of men who were still burdened over what happened in Vietnam—their role in it, the outcome, the way they were perceived for having participated. Within the "band of brothers" of a particular squadron or air group there were the "Vietnam vets" and then there were "all others." The newer officers and men had no idea what these older veterans had been through, and the older aviators often couldn't share what was on their hearts with the younger ones. It was clear to me that something needed to be done to help the healing process that has never happened.

Ralph took his experience as a Navy Reserve chaplain and his prior involvement with World Vision and set out to lead an organization that could fulfill his hope for healing. What he found when he got to Vietnam moved him deeply:

I've worked and traveled in more that sixty-five countries around the world where there are people in need. More often than not, the people are suffering because of a government or system that placed them in a position of peril. In Vietnam, the people had endured more than four decades of war and were now living under a system that could not meet the basic needs of the nation.

When I first went to Vietnam in 1988, their previous benefactors, the Soviet-bloc countries, were already in the process of collapse. There was rampant malaria, a decided lack of modern medical technology for the prevention or treatment of disease, and very little available to help the tens of thousands of those who had been so terribly wounded on both sides of the war.

I found dozens of hard-working doctors, nurses, orphanage directors, rehabilitation therapists, and health workers—all struggling, with almost nothing, to care for people who urgently needed help.

I took on the responsibility as CEO of International Aid with the belief that those of us who have the means to do so can and should help, though the people who need this help may live under a government that I do not approve of, or have beliefs different from mine. Just because the people of Vietnam live under a political system that is on the other side of my personal political spectrum doesn't mean that I shouldn't be there helping.

To deny people help for such a reason would be like refusing to help the child of a drug-addicted mother. In war, as in life, there are many victims of injustice. If my being in Vietnam with medicines and surgical equipment and X-ray machines helps heal bodies—and can help us as a nation heal some of the wounds we still suffer—then I am doing what I should.

From my experience as a military chaplain, I know the work that we are doing here in Vietnam is helping. It certainly isn't a sign of weakness. I've spent enough time with men and women in uniform to know that this is a mission for strong people, not weak ones.

It was clear to me during our April 1993 visit to Vietnam that Ralph and his team from International Aid are indeed making a difference.

During the trip, I asked him about how others perceived his work in Vietnam, and whether he was ever criticized for being one of the first American relief organizations involved in an "enemy country."

Look, I was a military chaplain, I fully understand the meaning of the word *enemy*. But I also know the meaning of those words: "Love your enemies, do good to those who hate you" (Luke

6:27), or "When a man's way pleases the LORD, he makes even his enemies to be at peace with him" (Proverbs 16:7 RSV).

International Aid's medical director, Dr. Jack Henderson, is an accomplished pediatrician who served as a Navy physician in the early 1960s. After sea duty, Dr. Henderson was given a port assignment in San Diego. It was there that he became involved in medical mission work as a volunteer in his off-duty hours across the border in the poorest part of Tijuana. More than twenty years later, Jack left a successful private medical practice to become IA's first full-time physician/medical director. He is understandably proud of the work that has been done in Vietnam.

We have had a lot of success with our prosthetics program in central Vietnam, based in Da Nang. Here in America, we take for granted that amputees can get artificial limbs. It is not so easy in Vietnam, and the number of those needing prostheses there is impossible to count.

As we traveled throughout Vietnam, those of us who had only recently met Jack were deeply affected by his "bedside manner." I'll never forget seeing him caress and gently examine grossly disfigured and retarded children in an orphanage we visited near Da Nang. His entire demeanor was one of caring and healing. Even to an old warrior it was easy to see in Jack Henderson a clear message of hope as well as the means to fulfill it.

One of International Aid's supporters, Bud Hoffman, fought in Vietnam's Central Highlands, near Pleiku, in the same area where my brother, Jack, served. Like Jack, he was in the U.S. Army; like me, Bud was there in 1968 and '69. Today, Bud is a successful businessman, but twice he's traveled back to Vietnam with International Aid to help deliver medicines and medical equipment. Bud was with us on our trip in April '93, and I saw him visibly moved by the plight of those in hospitals and orphanages. I asked what motivated him to give so generously of his time, energy, and resources.

"Ollie, these people were my enemies; the war you and I fought in didn't end the way we would have had it; but it didn't end for these people in a way that made their lives any better, either," he told me. "Look at the suffering we've seen here. It's not your fault or mine, and it certainly isn't the fault of the children we see in these hospitals or orphanages. But if we have the means to help now, and we don't, it sure *will* be our fault."

Bud Hoffman's thoughts are echoed by Bill Barta, IA's vice-president for operations. Bill graduated in 1958 from West Point and in spite of being the Most Valuable Player on the Army football team (my alma mater's arch rival!) I still like him. Bill served in Vietnam at the same time I was there, and he, too, had been in I Corps, assigned to the U.S. Army's Americal Division, near Chu Lai, south of Da Nang. Like Bud Hoffman and hundreds of other veterans of The War, Bill sees the work International Aid is doing in Vietnam as an important part of the healing that is so necessary to putting the past behind us.

As a combat veteran of Vietnam, I've seen the grief of a suffering people firsthand in what was then and is now one of the poorest parts of Asia. My military experience has opened my eyes to needs that many others never see. I've encountered the ravages of war in the bloody stumps of Vietnamese children and battered veterans. I feel the need to help with the same kind of daring you and I saw on the battlefield.

Now that the Russians have abandoned Vietnam, we have a grand opportunity to do things that were impossible before. We don't do these things out of guilt or shame, but because it's the right thing for us to do. We're directly involved in providing real help that's desperately needed, we're helping to shore up Christian pastors and the remnants of the Church, and we're doing it openly without any hidden agenda. The U.S. and Vietnamese governments both know what we're doing and how we're doing it. We seek neither profit nor political advantage.

If I can help International Aid be a forerunner and serve as an example to other like-minded organizations in Vietnam, then we will have furthered the process of reconciliation. I believe that if we work together, serving an old enemy, we can break down the barriers of thirty years of hatred.

As I learned firsthand on our 1993 trip back to my old battlegrounds, the work that Ralph Plumb undertook following his first trip in 1988 is indeed having the effect that Bill Barta described. Perhaps best of all from my perspective, International Aid is working closely with other relief organizations and has no "political baggage" from activities predating the end of the war.

For years, the only Americans the Vietnamese saw were those who had protested the war or who took an active role in undermining America's involvement in Vietnam. Some of these individuals and organizations maintained contacts and offices in Hanoi during the war and, after the collapse of the South Vietnamese government in 1975, established operations in what had been South Vietnam. To the Hanoi government the driving force behind these groups was always ideological and political even when they were offering help to clinics or hospitals.

There is a certain sense of wonder among the Vietnamese concerning groups, such as International Aid and Vets with a Mission, that came with an exclusively humanitarian purpose in 1988 as a result of General Vessey's mission. Many Vietnamese seem positively baffled by such NGOs.

One of our government "guides" asked me about them during our trip.

"You were a Marine here during the war?" he asked, almost as a statement of fact.

"Yes, I was," I replied.

"Then you are doing this because you feel bad about what you did here?" Again, a statement-question as though he knew the answer.

"No. I don't feel guilty about anything that I did here. I don't feel shame about what my country tried to do here. I am a Christian. I am here because I believe that Christians who have the means to give the kind of help your people so desperately need are supposed to do these kinds of things."

His only response was to nod his head and say, "I see."

I don't know whether he really did "see" and am not certain that he understood what I meant by being a "Christian," but at the very least he thought about it. A day later he took the opportunity to ask: "Why do Christians do these things?"

He was a former military man, and though too young to have fought in The War, I knew he would understand about "following orders." I said, "We Christians do these things because we're told to."

"You're told to? Who told you to?"

I gave him a copy of the New Testament printed in Vietnamese and said, "It's all in here. It's kind of like orders from our Commander in Chief."

I'll probably never know whether this official of the Vietnamese government, who was also very likely a member of their secret police, read what I gave him, but at least being there gave me the chance to pass on a copy of the Good Word.

I also hoped (but could not share with him) that what we were doing offered a chance for healing in my own country. The two of us shared no context for him to understand how the legacy of Vietnam had left so many festering wounds in America. He could clearly see the sick, maimed, and injured in his own country who were being healed by what we were doing, but how could I explain to him how helping Vietnam could also help people in my country, half a world away?

Ralph Plumb, Jack Henderson, Bud Hoffman, Bill Barta, and I aren't the only ones who have faced this dilemma. There are others who, thanks to General Vessey's vision, are wrestling with it. Many of them are veterans who, having served in that faraway, long-ago war, are now seizing the opportunity—with "daring" as Bill Barta put it—to further the healing in both places.

Bill Kimball was a mortarman with the U.S. Army's 1st Cavalry Division in Vietnam in 1968. After fewer than three months in country he was stricken with a serious tropical infection and was medevacked first to Japan, then to San Francisco, and hospitalized for nine months.

In 1988 Kimball established Vets With a Mission. "We had a straightforward, twofold purpose: I wanted to have an effect here at home as well as in Vietnam," said Bill when I asked him. "I particularly wanted to help American vets cope with the traumatic aftermath of the Vietnam War," he says. "And I felt that the best way to do that was to have vets reach out to others who are suffering even more devastating effects from the same events."

Vets with a Mission is a no-nonsense, roll-up-your-sleeves, get-it-done sort of operation. They specialize in taking veterans, and sometimes even their families, to Vietnam on missions to help the people in the land where we fought. Like International Aid, Vets with a Mission—VWAM—is a Christian-based organization. Their motto is taken from 2 Corinthians 5:18, "Called to a ministry of reconciliation." Over the past few years their projects have covered the full spectrum of needs in our old battleground. Recently they helped renovate an orphanage in Saigon that specializes in children with polio.

The vets on this mission repaired a therapy wading pool for polio victims, drilled a new well, and put in two new pumps. A new electrical system was put in, as were new lights, fans, and circuit boxes. A washing and laundry facility was added. Classrooms for children age five through seventeen, and an auditorium, were extensively rebuilt. VWAM bought a house near the orphanage to serve as a halfway shelter for older children who must leave the orphanage but have nowhere else to go. Today, they're engaged in helping several orphanages throughout the country.

In Ho Chi Minh City, Vets with a Mission has been financing the operation of a vocational rehabilitation center for teenagers. In 1992 and 1993 it was honored by the city government as the best-operated vocational rehab school in the city.

Troubled by the country's many amputees and cripples, Vets with a Mission joined with other organizations to help launch a comprehensive orthopaedic and surgical training program at Saigon's Center for Orthopaedic and Traumatology.

VWAM tries to involve veterans *and* their families in Vietnam, whether the work to be done is digging a trench or pulling teeth. Many of the U.S. vets engaged in this effort had received special training in the service and VWAM places a high premium on what we used to call "host country sensitivities"—knowing the local people's culture and way of life.

On one of his early missions back to Vietnam, Bill befriended Dr. Duong Quynh Hoa, a diminutive woman whose size might obscure her prominence as a highly respected physician. During The War she was the chief medical officer for the Viet Cong, and she has played a prominent role in the affairs of state since the fall of the South. When she learned about the veterans who chose to return to Vietnam with VWAM, Dr. Hoa was struck by the caring shown toward her people by former adversaries. She was a key to opening doors that previously had been closed, allowing VWAM to embark on a number of major projects to help the Vietnamese help themselves.

One of these projects is a medical center, in remote Phu Ngoc in the province of Dong Nai, which supports two satellite health clinics. American doctors, dentists, and various medical specialists—many of them Vietnam War vets—now come to Phu Ngoc to provide medical care for the local people and to train the Vietnamese so that they can provide up-to-date health care to their own people. Early in 1993, Hanoi designated this Vets with a Mission health station as the model rural-health-care center for all of Vietnam. The European Economic Community recently agreed to fund two additional health facilities in remote parts of Vietnam modeled on the one VWAM helped build at Phu Ngoc.

On a recent trip, one Vietnam vet, who was given lodging in Dr. Hoa's house, was moved by the irony of sleeping under her roof. Steve Hettick ate at her table. She helped him fix the mosquito netting over his bed. Hettick reflected later, "Who would have imagined twenty years ago that a combat trooper like me and the chief medical officer for the VC would be meeting as friends and sharing the same burden to heal the wounds of war? Twenty years ago I probably would have been decorated for killing this charismatic lady, but now we are 'brothers and sisters in arms.'"

• • •

How do those of us who have gone back to Vietnam end up returning there? By just about as many different routes as we once took through the jungles and rice paddies more than two decades ago. Roger Helle, a fellow Marine, arrived in Vietnam on his first tour of duty before I did, and he got back there before me as well. He is one of the many hundreds of war-era vets to have retraced their steps. Like so many others, his journey had a life-changing effect.

Roger first arrived in Vietnam when he was barely eighteen years old. Between 1966 and 1970 he served three tours there as a Marine infantryman. On 13 July 1970 he was caught in a firefight while out on patrol. The Western Union telegram sent to his parents read in part: ". . . SUFFERED MULTIPLE TRAUMATIC WOUNDS FROM SHRAPNEL AND BULLETS TO ALL EXTREMITIES. IN THE JUDGMENT OF THE ATTENDING PHYSICIAN, HIS CONDITION IS OF SUCH SEVERITY THAT HIS PROGNOSIS IS POOR. . . ." The young sergeant was medevacked back to the States. He spent six months in the hospital, then was medically retired by the military, but he recovered.

By the time Roger Helle's military career abruptly ended, he had faced just about every imaginable circumstance an infantryman might have encountered during The War. More than once he had a close brush with death. When a new sergeant arrived to take over his squad, Roger, who usually walked out in front of his unit as its point man on patrols, was moved to a spot in the middle. In a harrowing ambush that mowed down everyone else in the squad, Roger—who tried unsuccessfully to save two of his injured buddies—survived unscathed. Everyone else died.

Helle returned with a group of fellow vets in July 1990. With his wife and two children he walked the route of that fateful night when he alone emerged from the rice paddy alive. The four of them knelt as the local people looked on with tears in their eyes. Roger planted a small American flag in the soil in tribute—something we weren't allowed to do when we'd been there in combat—and led the group in prayer at the site where his buddies had perished. Today he is chairman of the board of Vets with a Mission.

When I went to Vietnam in 1968, I went with a purpose: to give the people of Vietnam a chance to live tranquil lives in peace. We weren't allowed to complete that mission. The consequence of our unfinished mission was a terrible tragedy for the people of Vietnam. Today, groups like International Aid and Vets with a Mission are trying to complete our original task. Instead of bombs and bullets, they are using bandages and antibiotics.

My return to Vietnam helped me see how simple acts of kindness go a long way toward healing old wounds and the scars borne by the Vietnamese people. Thanks to General Vessey's efforts and the hard work of people like Ralph Plumb and Bill Kimball, any American can work through one of several American organizations to channel relief to Vietnam. Perhaps equally important, what these organizations have done is to offer Americans a chance to heal our own hurts from the Vietnam War.

We have the means to do so, the need is great, and the goodwill we would reap would be extraordinary. It also happens to be the right thing to do.

What would happen if veterans' groups, churches, synagogues, and other organizations adopted a province, a hospital, or orphanage? Is it too far-fetched to dream that a major American hospital could open up a "branch" in Vietnam? Are there families who would be willing to take a "vacation with a purpose" in Vietnam, working with an NGO on a particular project?

Could we begin to see news reports of a new wave of caring Americans going to Vietnam to help rebuild a nation that most of us know only as a battlefield?

This book began with a cry for help from a platoon in trouble. The fighting is over now, the members of that platoon who survived are trying to make ends meet as mechanics, teachers, cops, truck drivers, factory workers, and even a dentist. Today, most are good family men with good jobs and nice homes. But Vietnam is still in trouble. For the Vietnamese children who reached out to us, for their parents, for the Vietnamese who fought alongside us and against us, for our own veterans still in hospitals, to honor those who died there or who are still missing—it's time to accept one more mission.

If your enemy is hungry, feed him; if he is thirsty, give him something to drink.
Romans 12:20

EPILOGUE

Narnia Farm, Virginia: 1 September 1993

TWENTY-FIVE YEARS AGO I LEFT THE UNITED STATES for The War in Vietnam. I was then a brand new, bright-eyed, bushy-tailed, newlywed, 2d Lieutenant of Marine Infantry. Nobody I knew then questioned why I was going. They knew. I had graduated from the U.S. Naval Academy; I was a Marine. There was a war on. It was expected.

This year I went back to Vietnam. The War there is over. I am now a middle-aged, bifocaled, gray-haired, husband of one and father of four. Many friends and colleagues questioned me, "Why go back to Vietnam?" They couldn't understand. "There's nothing that anyone can do that will make any difference," they said.

Most of those who made those kinds of com-

294

ments had not gone to Vietnam, did not lose someone in The War, did not have to wait patiently while someone they loved was there, or did not leave something of themselves in that faraway place so very long ago.

Those who had done these things did not ask, "Why go back?" They understood.

Betsy, my best friend, my wife of twenty-five years this November, the mother of the four children that the good Lord loaned us, understood. She had worried and waited through a very long year of The War in 1968 – 69 while I served as an infantry platoon leader in 3d Marine Division. The War was why I was not there when she gave birth to our first child. And The War was why she threatened to leave me in 1974, after I had volunteered to extend my second tour of duty in the 3d Marine Division. And when I returned, she relented and helped me deal with the deep melancholy I felt about the end of The War inasmuch as the country I had fought for abandoned the country I had fought in.

For nearly two decades Betsy helped me carry the burden I felt for the terrible "waste" of Vietnam. She knew how it had affected my perspective on so many things—from training other Marines, to my assignment at the White House, to the company I cofounded that employs so many refugees from that war. And she sensed the need I felt to somehow try to complete what we had started but left unfinished so long ago. This book is about finishing that task, healing old wounds, and offering help where it is desperately needed.

This book is also a tribute:

—To the 58,191 men and eight women whose names are etched on that long black wall in Washington;

—To the 2,260 Americans who are missing or unaccounted for in Southeast Asia or its surrounding waters;

—To the 2.9 million men and 11,500 women who served in Vietnam and Southeast Asia during The War;

—To the families of those of us who served there, who waited then, and those who wait today

I was privileged to lead—and be led by—some of the finest men that this country has ever called to defend it. They were not the pot-headed marauders that have been depicted in much of our media and in far too many books and movies. They were, instead, good and brave and decent young men—who served in an unpopular war because their country asked them to.

So much has been distorted and twisted about that experience that our children, who are inheriting the long, sad legacy of Vietnam, deserve another perspective. I have written this book in part so that America's next generation, my children among them, will better know the brave men I was blessed to lead—and who led me—and those we fought for and then abandoned to tragedy—the people of Vietnam.

For my service in that war, some have called me a hero. I have never thought of myself as such, nor called myself one. The men I served with were the real heroes—they fought and bled and died in the mud, wet, heat, cold, and fatigue because they believed that what they were doing was right. Not one of the Marines and sailors I was with in Vietnam thought that we would win all the battles only to lose the war. Yet that is precisely what happened.

In the end, we sent our sons to be maimed and crippled and to die for naught because the political leaders of this country lost their will. There was no lack of courage or skill on the battlefield. The lack of fortitude was solely in the corridors of power in Washington. The very people who sent a generation of young men off to war lost faith in themselves, the ideals of this blessed land, and in so doing, condemned millions to exile or worse.

My hope is that this book will, in some small way, help to serve as a reminder that we should never again sacrifice our youth to a cause and then abandon them to nothing more than a stark memorial on the Mall in our capital. Nor should we ever again commit to help a people overcome tyranny or oppression and then desert them. For if we do again to others what we did in Vietnam, we will invite the end of a way of life that has inspired the people of this planet for two centuries.

Part of this book is about quiet courage—not mine, but the courage of those I have been blessed to be around most of my life; the courage to do what one believes to be right—even when all the odds are against it. It's that kind of quiet courage that Matthew's gospel (8:5 – 13) describes in the Roman centurion who risks ridicule and rejection, perhaps even being charged with treason, by walking up to Jesus and asking Him to heal his sick servant.

I spent two decades among men like that Roman centurion. One of them, a Marine lieutenant colonel, had the faith and courage to kneel in the dirt to pray for me when I had seriously injured my back in 1978. And because Lieutenant Colonel John Grinalds, USMC, was willing to risk rejection, misunderstanding, and ridicule, I had the chance to feel the healing power of that same Jesus that Matthew wrote about, and then to come to know Him in a deeply personal way.

That experience convinces me that all hurts can be healed, no matter how deep, even those wounds from Vietnam. Some will want to wait for governments to act. Others will say that nothing we do now will make any difference. Still others are going to say the hurts are, even now, too raw to heal, or that the anger burns too deeply to quench. But having been back there this year, I don't believe any of that.

What I do believe is that this nation we live in has been blessed with bounty beyond measure for a reason. And part of that reason is so that we can, as our means allow, reach out to help others in ways that no others can. And the people of Vietnam certainly need that help as much as anybody on earth.

Should we do that out of some sense of "guilt" over the past? Not at all. I feel no guilt over what we did, or tried to do, in Vietnam. But I would feel that I had done less than I could to honor the sacrifice of so many if my countrymen continue to think of Vietnam as an "experience," or as a "syndrome," or as The War.

Thankfully some, like the organizations and individuals I met there and have described in this book, are already engaged in the effort to help heal the wounds of America's longest war. But much more needs to be done. There are seventy million people in Vietnam, most of whom, despite the past, sincerely like the people of America. What we need now is a broader willingness to accept the challenge that Vietnam offers. Who will help? There are many of us who served there who could pitch in one more time and thereby honor those with whom we served. All that's needed are enough Americans of faith and courage who know that we were not put here to simply endure the future; we are here to change it for the good. We are not creatures in some desperately uneven contest; we are all sons and daughters of Adam and Eve, and we are supposed to determine our own fate, not have it dictated by the past. And, finally, we have each been given unique gifts and talents that we are supposed to use to glorify the Lord God who made us and who sent His Son to save us all.

OLN
Narnia Farm
Virginia
1 September 1993

GLOSSARY

ACTUAL: Term used by the military in radio-call signs to identify the leader of a particular unit. For example, "Kilo One Actual" is the call sign for the Platoon Leader, 1st Platoon, Company K.

AIR STRIKE: The delivery of ordnance from aircraft against ground targets. *See* Close Air Support.

ANTENNA FARM: A term frequently used to refer to the cluster of radio antennas that usually move with or near a commander. During movement, it was relatively easy to identify the location of a battalion commander from the radio antennas that were usually nearby. Antenna farms were good places to stay away from in Vietnam.

APC: An armored personnel carrier—a lightly armored, tracked vehicle used to carry infantry troops. Ours were M-111s. In Vietnam, U.S. Army and South Vietnamese Army mechanized units used in flat terrain and along major roads. In February 1969 I managed to lose most of the M-111 APCs that were on temporary loan to the Marines from the Army. I don't believe they loaned us any more.

ARC LIGHT: The code name for saturation air strikes against North Vietnamese and Viet Cong ground forces and installations by B-52 strategic bombers that were guided to their targets by radio or radar beacons. An Arc Light could make the ground shake like an earthquake. We used to wonder how anything could live through such a raid. It was 1993 before I found out.

ARVN: Army of the Republic of Vietnam, the South Vietnamese Army. The term ARVN was commonly used to refer to any South Vietnamese military unit or individual soldier.

BONUS INCENTIVE PLAN: A term used to refer to a carefully prescribed financial ritual that got things done in the free-enterprise system that existed in Vietnam. In most other places it is called extortion.

B-52: An American long-range heavy bomber. Those who flew these enormous machines were the envy of garden-variety soldiers and Marines who walked to the line of departure—until some of the pilots and crews began showing up as POWs at the Hanoi Hilton.

BLT: A Marine battalion landing team. A task-organized Marine amphibious unit of about 2,200 men. A BLT is formed by attaching specialized units to an Infantry Battalion; usually armor, artillery, amphibious assault vehicles, and other combat support and service-support units that enable the BLT to assault the beach and conduct self-sustaining operations against enemy forces ashore. A BLT is not a sandwich.

"CHICOM": Short for "Chinese Communist." The North Vietnamese often used wooden-handled hand grenades that we referred to as "ChiCom grenades." Thankfully, these weapons had a very high malfunction rate. *See* "Dud."

CHOPPER: Short for helicopter. These noisy, unsafe, unstable, life-threatening, life-saving, absolutely lovely, green machines were flown by the most courageous men in the world. Pilots who fly choppers are known as Rotor Heads.

CLAYMORE MINE: A directional, command-detonated, anti-personnel mine packed with explosives and steel pellets. The U.S. version of this device used electrically detonated C-4 plastic explosives to spray hundreds of steel pellets at an approaching enemy.

CLOSE AIR SUPPORT: What a Marine in contact wants most of all. *See* Airstrike. *See* Contact.

CONTACT: Term used to refer to an ambush, firefight, attack, or other engagement with the enemy.

DMZ: The Demilitarized Zone. The "Z" was a four-mile-wide buffer of land that straddled the Ben Hai River and roughly followed the 17th Parallel that separated North and South Vietnam. It was established in the Geneva Accords of 1954. It didn't even show on the NVA maps we captured.

DUD: Short for "did not detonate." Term used by troops to refer to a bomb, artillery round, grenade, rocket, mine, or other explosive device that did not go off when it was supposed to. Also pertains to individuals who do not think too fast; as in, "Jones is a dud."

F4 PHANTOM: A high-performance, two-seat twin-engine, jet tactical fighter aircraft used by the

U.S. Air Force, Navy, and Marines. The aircraft was also employed to deliver air-to-ground ordnance such as bombs, rockets, and guns against North Vietnamese and Viet Cong targets. Hated by the enemy. Loved by Marines and soldiers in contact.

FIREBASE: A well-prepared position, usually a hilltop that was scraped clear of vegetation, and had numerous revetments and emplacements for artillery pieces and mortars. Firebases were usually subjected to intense enemy fire since the NVA and VC quickly figured out that we would put them on the highest hill around. North Vietnamese and VC gunners probably referred to them as large, vulnerable, stationary targets.

.50 CAL: A belt-fed, heavy-caliber machine gun, usually fired from a wheel-mounted tripod or vehicle. Though designed primarily as an anti-aircraft weapon, they were also used by both sides in defensive positions to provide direct fire against ground attacks.

FO: Forward observer. Usually a field artillery lieutenant who moved with an infantry unit and had the mission of calling and adjusting artillery fire.

HO CHI MINH TRAIL: The name given by U.S. and South Vietnamese forces to the extensive road and trail network that was used by the NVA to supply their units in the south. This interconnecting complex of roads and trails extended over portions of four countries: North Vietnam, South Vietnam, Laos, and Cambodia.

IV: Short for "intravenous." In Vietnam, field corpsmen and medics carried bottles of saline solution or lactate fluid to use immediately after a man was wounded, in an effort to reduce shock and compensate for loss of blood.

LAAW or LAW: "Light anti-armor weapon," a one-shot, armor-piercing, shoulder-fired missile in a disposable, fiberglass tube.

M-60: A belt-fed, 7.62mm NATO standard, medium machine gun used by American and Allied forces. Though the Marine Corps Table of Organization (T/O) authorized this weapon to be issued only to the Weapons Platoon of an Infantry Company, three M-60s could usually be found in each Rifle Platoon.

MEDEVAC: Short for "medical evacuation" by air, usually by helicopter, sometimes by plane.

NVA: North Vietnamese Army. Commonly used by troopers to refer to any North Vietnamese unit or individual soldier.

0-1: A small, single-engine, two-seat, high-wing observation aircraft used to call in and adjust artillery, naval gunfire, and close-air support.

POINT: Also "point man." The lead man on a patrol. The man at the head of a formation or column.

RIF: Reconnaisance-in-force. Unlike a normal reconnaisance mission to observe the enemy but avoid contact, an RIF mission is heavily armed and seeks to engage an enemy force, fix it in position, and call in even larger units to destroy it.

RPG: Rocket-propelled grenade. RPGs were fired from Soviet- and Chinese-made, shoulder-held launchers. Designed as a close-range, anti-tank weapon, RPGs were frequently used by the NVA against our infantry units.

STARLIGHT SCOPE: A night-vision telescope that uses ambient light to see the enemy in darkness.

THERMITE GRENADE: An incendiary device that produces an intense fire, hot enough to melt metal. We frequently used these grenades in Vietnam to destroy captured enemy weapons and equipment that could not be evacuated.

VT FUSE: Variable Time Fuse. Used on an artillery or mortar projectile to cause the round to detonate at a preselected height above the ground. This fuse was effective against troops in the open or deployed in dug-in positions without overhead cover.

WILLIE PETE(R): White phosphorous artillery, mortar or rocket round, which burns intensely and creates a large plume of white smoke when it detonates. Used to mark targets for airstrikes and to mask movement of friendly troops from enemy observation.

Z: Abbreviation for *demilitarized zone*.

HOW CAN YOU HELP?

THROUGHOUT THIS BOOK I HAVE CALLED UPON Americans to finish in Vietnam what the war didn't do: give the Vietnamese people a better life. In my opinion, the best way to do that is to join hands with any of the 150 or more American humanitarian agencies who are already working in Vietnam. For a complete list of these agencies, contact the State Department.

Because my friends at International Aid helped me so much on my return to Vietnam, I would like to tell you a little more about their work there.

International Aid is a Christian, humanitarian organization dedicated to enabling, empowering, and encouraging those who serve the poor and needy. They work in collaboration with thousands of individuals, churches, corporations, and organizations providing food, health, and hope to those in need around the world. They have five main program areas: emergency relief, development programs (helping people become self-sufficient), medical programs, mission assistance (support for missionaries and relief workers), and domestic programs (assistance to America's needy).

International Aid's work in Vietnam preceeded the war and resumed in 1988 when General John Vessey helped secure agreements between Vietnam and the United States to allow humanitarian exchanges with U.S.-based private voluntary organizations (PVOs). International Aid's president, Ralph E. Plumb, was a member of one of the first American delegations allowed to visit Vietnam after the war. Since 1988, International Aid has provided more than nineteen major shipments of surgical and hospital supplies, medicines, and technical medical equipment to south, central, and north Vietnam. I saw firsthand some of their equipment in the hospitals we visited.

Currently, International Aid is raising funds for major program expansion in Vietnam. In addition to their ongoing work in providing medical equipment and supplies, they are planning some exciting new programs that the Vietnamese desparately need. For example, for a relatively minor investment they can provide scholarships, internships, and exchange programs for Vietnamese doctors and medical students. They are also planning to fund economic development projects that will enable the industrious Vietnamese people to set up self-sustaining businesses that contribute to the economy.

One thing I have learned from my own Vietnamese employees is that they don't want handouts—just a chance. International Aid is in a key position to give thousands of Vietnamese that chance.

If you would like more information about how you can help International Aid with their work in Vietnam, or how you might travel to Vietnam on a sponsored tour, contact:

Ralph E. Plumb, President
International Aid Inc.
17011 W. Hickory
Spring Lake, MI 49456
Phone: (616) 846-7490
FAX: (616) 846-3842 275

INDEX